The solitary Witch's Green Book

Basic Witch spells & journaling
for your everyday magic practice

Beatrix Minerva Linden

The information contained in this book is not meant to substitute the advice of a doctor. If you have health issues consult your medical care provider. Herbs and essential oils can be potent and counteract with certain drugs and medication. They should be used with extreme care and in case of doubt double check their safety with your physician. Please use candles and sharp objects with care and under your responsibility to avoid cuts, fires and other accidents. All the information in this book is given subjectively and exclusively for entertainment purposes. The author can't be held responsible for any damage or loss caused by the use or misuse of the contents of this book or by any mistakes in it. None of the information contained in this book is meant to be legal or financial advice. Readers agree to use this book and its contents at their own risk and responsibility. Results are not guaranteed in any way.

THIS BOOK IS NOT SUITABLE FOR CHILDREN.

We would like to express our thanks to the creator of the font Du Bellay from Daniel's fonts (available at goodreasonblog.com), which is used throughout the book.

To my mother.

Contents

Contents v

INTRODUCTION: This Witch's Life............. 8

How to work with this book 11

CHAPTER 1: *Let's Do Some Magic*...............13

    Day 1: A Magic Journal.....................................13

    Day 2: Could You Be A Witch?.....................15

    Day 3: Finding Your Path..............................18

    Day 4: What Kind Of Witch Are You?........21

    Day 5: A Witch's Code of Ethics 28

    First Weekend: Cleansing and Scrying..........31

CHAPTER 2: A Witch's Box 34

    Day 6: Wands 34

    Day 7: The Elements.......................................38

    Day 8: Ritual Knives.......................................40

    Day 9: Divination tools...................................44

    Day 10: Creating An Altar 48

    Second Weekend: Hugging Trees..................51

CHAPTER 3: Magic Ingredients 53

    Day 11: Candle Magic 53

    Day 12: Herbs...56

    Day 13: Crystals and Chakras........................59

    Day 14: Tarot card spells 64

    Day 15: Banishing spells 67

Third Weekend: Meditation Quick Start Guide 69

CHAPTER 4: The World Around You 73

Day 16: The Moon And The Goddess 73

Day 17: The Magic of The Moon 76

Day 18: The Power of the Sun 80

Day 19: Planets and Stars: the World of Astrology 84

Day 20: Numerology 90

Fourth Weekend: Animal Companions 92

CHAPTER 5: Spellwork 101 95

Day 21: Cleansing 96

Day 22: Grounding and Shielding 101

Day 23: Magical Symbols 103

Day 24: Casting A Circle 107

Day 25: Using Correspondences 110

Fifth Weekend: The Principles of Manifestation 111

CHAPTER 6: Spellwork II 114

Day 26: Sigil Magic 115

Day 27: Freezing Spells and Cord Cutting. 117

Day 28: Money Spells 120

Day 29: Spells to Assist with Healing 122

Day 30: Love Spells 126

Sixth Weekend: Creating a Magic Pouch ... 127

CHAPTER 7: Wrapping It All Up (In Silk) .. 129

CHAPTER 8: Useful Lists And Tables 130

Runes Keywords 130

Tarot Keywords 132

Tables Of Correspondences 138

About The Author 140

INTRODUCTION:
This Witch's Life

Do you believe in Witches?

What if I told you Witches[1] are living among us today? What if **you and I** were one of them?

When I was younger, I used to think I was a little peculiar, but I never pinpointed why. If you saw me, the word *Witch* wouldn't be the first one to cross your mind. I am just a plain girl in a t-shirt and jeans, who mostly rides the bus, or a bicycle if the weather is nice. I'm not much of a broom rider. Flying is not my thing, to tell the truth. I don't really do curses, let alone wear a black pointed hat. Except for Halloween, maybe, although some of us prefer to call it *Samhain*.

Before I moved to *The Land of Eternal Winter*, I used to work in a cubicle in a tall skyscraper, send postcards to my Catholic grandma and spend my (scarce) free time watering cactuses and reading romantic novels.

"What?", will you ask, *"do you mean you are a Witch? And you don't eat children? You mean you don't worship demons and run away from garlic?"* (Garlic should be more of a problem for vampires, by the way).

Hopefully, if you are reading this book, you already know about modern Witches, who are mostly kind and harmless people, who don't drink blood nor do they have wart-infested noses and chins. They are not a bunch of pale, black-haired females: Witches come in all genders, colors and

---

[1] *You may notice the words Witch and Witchcraft have been capitalized throughout the book. This has been done on purpose, in order to distinguish a Witch, as a wise woman, from a witch, when used as a derogatory term in children's tales and colloquial speech. This way we have tried to give Witches back the respect they deserve.*

nationalities.

Are you a Witch?

Have you ever wondered? Would you like to try the Witch's life? This book will help you bring magic into your life. You will just need to invest a few minutes every day. This will be a quick and informative read, and hopefully an entertaining one, too. In a couple of weeks, many secrets of Witchcraft will be revealed to you. Consider this a book and a workbook in one, which will take you step by step from magical layman to proper Witch. After you finish all the exercises, you will have your own magic journal, or *book of shadows*, and enough knowledge to keep walking your path in the direction you decide.

So, is this the right book for you?

- If you are interested in magic, spells, and Witchcraft, but you don't really know where to start, this book will help you find your path.
- If you don't know any other Witches, or you prefer to practice Witchcraft on your own for privacy or schedule reasons, I encourage you to give this book a chance.
- If you are interested in magic, but you are not sure you want to be a Wiccan, a Druid, a Pagan, or just practice magic sporadically, you will like this book.
- If you are interested in solitary traditional Witchcraft, Christian Witchcraft, atheistic Witchcraft or any other branch of Witchcraft apart from mainstream *magick*, this book will help you get an easy-to-understand overview of the magic world

and its customs. You don't have to turn magic into your religion if you don't want to. You can, but you don't *have to*. You can change your mind later, too. Witchcraft is not a one-way street. There are as many types of Witches as drops of rain, all similar, but all different.

A concise, green book of Witchcraft

Green is the color of nature and the color of growth. Just like trees grow tall from a tiny seed, we, Witches, expand our consciousness every day. One day you hear the call, you get a sign which lights the first spark, and that is how your spiritual quest starts. This ends up being the first seed. Once you start walking the Witch's path, you are able to grow as tall as you decide. Your knowledge branches out, and you start to discover the many sides of magic. Let nature, the plants, the Moon and the rest of celestial bodies be your allies in this magical adventure you are about to embark on.

Now put on your reading glasses, make yourself a nice cup of tea and come on board. You can even put on a black pointed hat, too. I promise I will tell no one!

How to work with this book

This book can be used as **a six-week course, which will get you acquainted with the foundations of traditional magic, divination, spellwork, and much more**. You will find an informative passage for each day, from Monday to Friday, followed by a brief practical task to reinforce what you have learnt. If you tend to be forgetful, just set a reminder on your mobile phone, every day at the same hour, to read the chapter of the day. Ideally, start on a Monday morning or Sunday evening.

Once you finish working with this manual, you will have started your own *book of shadows* and will be able to cast your own spells. You will get to know many new and useful concepts. And the best part: this will take you just a few minutes per day to achieve.

All beginner Witches can benefit from this book, but medium-level practitioners will probably find useful information in its pages, too: the whole book is very concise, and the information is concentrated and clearly explained.

In order to use this book you will need a journal. Any notebook will do, although many Witches like to hand craft their own journals or find a beautiful vintage notebook they will be able to treasure many years and even pass on to their children and grandchildren. This journal will become what most Witches like to call their *book of shadows*.

If you want, you can get the companion notebook ***The Solitary Witches Green Journal***, by the same author, which matches this book and its contents.

It can also be a good idea to read the whole book before you start, because you will get a quick overview and will be able to collect your supplies slowly (don't worry, there isn't anything too fancy, rare or expensive on our supply list). Afterwards, you can complete the assignments, a little at a time. You will soon realize **how easy it is to be a Witch on a budget**: most of the things you need are already in your pantry or near your home.

One more thing: **even if a task seems too simple, it's in there for a reason. Don't skip any of them!** Follow the plan outlined in this book and, after six weeks or less, you will be a practicing Witch, if you wish to.

CHAPTER 1:
Let's Do Some Magic

Day 1: A Magic Journal

During this first week we will reflect on your magical path, and what you expect to achieve by practicing Witchcraft. Start on a Monday, or even better, read each day's assignment on the evening of the day before. I will give you five tasks, one for each weekday, and then you will have the whole weekend to catch up with what you didn't finish during the previous days. Don't worry, it may sound like a lot of work, but it's not.

The only thing you will need for now is a notebook and a pen. You can call this notebook **a journal, or a _book of shadows,_** if you prefer. A book of shadows is a Witch's journal, where she[2] (or he) compiles her experiences, her beliefs and her spells. It is like a unique, personal encyclopedia of magic. Books of shadows are called so because, in the past, they had to remain hidden, thus "in the shadows", to prevent them from being discovered by nosy neighbors and visitors. Being exposed might have been dangerous (or even fatal) for many Witches. I prefer to call my book of shadows a _journal,_ as I am lucky and I don't need to hide it anymore. I also use it daily to

---

[2] _I may use the pronoun "she" when referring to Witches, but I hope this book will still be enjoyed by Witches of all genders, no matter what their preferred pronouns are._

reflect on magic, my life's happenings and the divination methods I like to use, like you would use a journal.

Your task for today is to get hold of a notebook: it can be as humble or as baroque as you decide.

- Decorate the cover if you want to.
- On the first page, write today's date and the following information:

This journal (or book of shadows) belongs to... (Write your name, your date and place of birth and any other personal data you would wish to add. If you have a *craft name*[3], or revere a certain deity/saint/entity, you can mention them too).

- Try to create an introduction to your journal by answering the following questions:
  - What is a Witch? (In your own words).
  - What is magic?
  - If you have ever tried to practice magic, or do a spell in the past, write about your experience and its outcome. When was that? What was the purpose of the spell? Where did you find the spell, and do you think it worked?

Note: from now on, try to leave at least half blank page at the end of each entry, because you might like to add new information and ideas as you progress. If you don't know the answers, you can just write what your gut feeling suggests you, or leave a blank space for later.

---

[3] *A craft name is the name you use as a Witch. When Witches work together, they call each other by their craft name. This helps them keep their anonymity (and their safety). In coven (Witch circles) settings, craft names are given by the coven to the new Witches. If you work alone, you can still have a craft name you connect well with. You can meditate on it and decide what your craft name should be. You can choose one which describes your path, what is sacred to you, etc. Of course, you can still be a Witch and use only your given name, there is nothing wrong with that.*

Day 2: Could You Be A Witch?

Have you ever met a *real* Witch? (What's that, anyway?).

Maybe you have, but you haven't even noticed! Many people need a while to come to terms with the word *Witch* itself. Ugly, evil Witches' clichés are deeply ingrained in our collective minds, fed by centuries of misinformation and defamatory folk tales. You might go through a hard time accepting the name *Witch* as your own, and it's understandable. For me, all this changed when I met Claire, back in my twenties.

I was still a student and had a part-time job in a coffee shop. That's where I met my best friend at the time: Claire. She was the opposite from me: blonde, bold and outgoing. Out of the three waitresses in our coffee shop, she was the only one who seemed satisfied with her life and completely uninterested in gossiping and backstabbing the rest of her co-workers. She had an almost visible aura and exuded positive energy wherever she went. She was kind to everyone, but she let no one intimidate her. We both loved nature, ecology, and were fascinated by the feminine side of things. It's not strange that we became friends. Her peaceful but decided ways fascinated me, and one day I gathered the courage to ask her why she was so different. She looked at me in surprise, and said:

"I am a Witch, if that's what you mean. I thought you knew!", and she showed me her pentacle pendant like it was the most obvious thing in the world. To be honest, back then I thought it was just a cute silver star.

Claire became my friend and my mentor, and the first proud Witch I ever met.

So, are you a Witch?

What about you? If you are reading this book, you might wonder whether you might be a Witch, too. The good news is, **there is only one condition to becoming a Witch: you have to want to.** That's it. No tests to pass, no-one to prove your *witchiness* to. Just lots of learning on your horizon.

Sadly, many Witches nowadays are still afraid to present

themselves openly. In some communities, saying you are a Witch is enough to bring back echoes of the Burning Times, when many innocent people died horrible deaths for that very reason. Most of them didn't even have anything to do with Witchcraft. They were just ordinary mothers and daughters, sometimes herbal healers, and very rarely true practicing Witches.

True Witches, the ones we will deal with in this book, are no more evil than anyone else. The word *Witch* is used to refer to a wise woman (or man), a healer, a helper, a spellcaster, an herbalist or an intermediary between the realm of the living and the one of spirits. Siberian and Native American shamans, *curanderos*, *bruixas*, Italian *streghe* and even the midwives from the past might be considered Witches by some. In old European societies, Witches were thought to be always female, but there are male Witches, too. Nowadays, many men practice magic and call themselves Witches or magicians.

There are still countries in the world where it is forbidden to practice Witchcraft, due to the assumption that magic is synonymous with evil and the works of the devil. Hopefully you are not in one of them. It's time we change the negative stigma attached to the word *Witch*. Let's start by avoiding expressions such as *"That woman is a Witch! She stole my husband"* or *"I hate that Witch!"*. Being called a Witch shouldn't be an insult, but an honor. Or, at least, a neutral, descriptive noun, just like *dentist* or *gardener*.

If you find the word Witch scary and have a problem referring to yourself as one, you can practice in front of the mirror. Just look at yourself and ask your reflection:

"Am I a Witch?".

Trust me: one day, your reflection will look back at you, just like Claire looked at me, and answer confidently:

*"Yes! You **are** a great Witch!"*

Today's task

Meditate on the following questions. Try to remember situations in your life which could apply and write them down in your book of shadows.

Envision yourself, your childhood and your recent past.

- Do you think you might possess psychic abilities? Describe them.
- Were you one of those dreamy children, who can get lost in their imagination to the point of astral traveling?
- Have you always felt older than your age?
- Do you sometimes know things nobody has told you and have a strong intuition?
- Have you ever had prophetic dreams?
- Do you sometimes perceive someone beside you, or following you, despite being sure there is nobody there?
- Are you empathic, can you sense other people's sadness, or happiness, as if it were your own?
- Do you feel drawn to esoteric matters, divination methods, crystals or healing herbs?
- Do you thrive in natural settings and love to care for the rest of living beings?
- Do you like to help others and do others come to you often for help?
- Last but not least, why are you reading this book?

These, and many others, are common traits of many Witches. If you have answered yes to a few questions, this book might interest you, so keep reading! The magic is waiting for you.

Day 3: Finding Your Path

Wiccan, traditional or something else?

When I was starting out, most newly converted Witches seemed to choose the Wiccan path. My friend, Claire, was the first person I met who talked openly about Witchcraft, and she happened to be a Wiccan, too. For a while I thought I would become one, just like her. But there are as many paths as Witches on this planet, and not all of us are meant to follow a Wiccan or even Pagan spiritual path. Maybe you are a Wiccan at heart, and maybe you are not. I know I am not, and I also know that it doesn't make me any less of a Witch. Maybe you just want to practice magic, and keep worshipping your God(s) or Goddesses, or Saints, just like you have been doing your whole life. Maybe you feel called to convert to a nature-based, Pagan faith. It's your choice and no-one else's. All choices are valid and deserve respect. I would like to offer you an overview of the different heathen spiritual paths out there, because, if nothing else, you will meet other Witches one day, and you will need to know the differences between Wiccan, traditional, Asatru, etc.

It is important to differentiate between magic and religion, as they are not the same thing. Right now most books about Witchcraft are being published by Wiccan authors. Witchcraft is not a religion, at least not necessarily. But Wicca is a religion, although it might differ from the ones most of us grew up with as children. This means there are certain guidelines, traditions and belief systems you have to follow if you want to be a Wiccan. Most Wiccans belong to a coven, that is, a group of like-minded individuals, who gather to celebrate, keep each other company and honor their God and Goddess. There are High Priests and High Priestess, and levels of initiation one can achieve inside a coven. Sometimes there are entry requirements, and covens don't just accept anyone who knocks at their door. Some covens are more open, others are more secretive. There are solitary Wiccans, too. They don't belong to covens or respond to any High Priests, but they share the same beliefs as the rest of members of this religion. Wiccans practice magical rituals, and they include their religious beliefs in their magical rituals. So it is safe to state that all Wiccans are Witches, and that Witchcraft is their religion.

But not all Witches are Wiccan. Witches can belong to any religion, or to none. There are Pagan, Christian, agnostic and even atheist Witches. **Witches are, simply put, people who practice magic**, or, as some people like to spell it, *magick* with a *K* at the end. The extra *K* differentiates *magick*, as a ritual or a form of spirituality, from magic, the one performed by illusionists and stage artists, consisting in hidden tricks. In this book I prefer to use the original spelling of the word, as I am not a fan of spelling innovations, but it will be helpful for you to know both versions exist and why.

Wiccans are members of a relatively new religion, created as a revival of ancient cults which honor a God and a Goddess, the male and female counterparts of all energies in our planet. Different Wiccan communities honor different male and female deities: some choose gods from the Roman pantheon, while others prefer the Greek or the Egyptian ones. To Wiccans, all Gods and Goddesses are different parts of the same whole: they can accept other people's Gods existence, and don't consider their Gods the only true ones. Their religion doesn't exclude or deny the existence of other people's deities. Wiccans have a set of tools and rituals, and celebrate certain holidays every year, which are called *Sabbats* and *Esbats*, and together form the holidays of the Wheel of the Year.

Traditional Witches, on the other hand, have existed for centuries, in many cultures and religions. They, unlike Wiccans, rarely consider magic a religion. They may or may not honor a God and a Goddess: some believe in an only God, or Goddess, or other deities, or none. Some celebrate the same holidays as other Pagans, but others don't. They may or may not use magic tools. They may or may not pray. Most of them don't respond to High Priests and Priestess, and follow their own, personal spiritual path, which may be unique and totally different from other Witches'. You would be surprised to find out there are even Christian Witches out there. Some might not dare to call themselves Witches because of the connotations associated with this word, but they don't mind casting spells whenever needed. Do you know anyone like this? I do. Truth to be told, many religions consider the practice of magic a sin, so this kind of traditional Witches usually have to do much soul-searching before deciding to go this route. **For traditional Witches, unlike Wiccans, religious choices are completely independent from their practice.**

Some people like to call themselves magicians. This term is usually reserved for those who work with ceremonial magic, as practiced by certain secret metaphysical societies. Ceremonial magic is sometimes called "high magic", an expression I dislike because it somehow infers that Witches practice a lower, less valuable kind of magic. For that reason, I try to avoid the use of that word, and stick to the expression *ceremonial* or *ritualistic* magic when referring to magical orders and hermetic societies.

A Final Word About Beginner Witches and Wicca:

For a beginner Witch, it may be simpler to follow the structure found in Wiccan religion. There is also plenty of available reading materials on Wicca, so this seems to be the start point for many Witches nowadays. It seems to me, though, that there is some confusion among young Witches on this subject. **Traditional Witchcraft gives Witches almost total freedom of choice. This can be scary** for a beginner, but hopefully this book will serve you as a guide while finding your path.

Your task for today

You will find a list of questions at the end of the page. These can be quite hard to answer, so don't worry if you don't have an answer for each of them right now. Mankind has been trying to discover the key to spirituality since the dawn of time, so just do your best. You may find your beliefs change with time, as you mature and accumulate life experiences.

There are no wrong answers, as this concerns just you and your faith (or lack thereof). The idea is to help you find out more about yourself by writing about these things.

If, for any reasons, you don't feel safe writing down the answers, just ponder them in your head.

Make a new entry in your journal about finding your path, think about your spiritual beliefs and write a short paragraph including the following subjects:

- What religious beliefs were you brought up with?
- Do you believe in a Higher Power or a God or in different dimensions of existence?
- Do humans have an immortal soul? What is that, anyway?
- Are your spiritual needs fulfilled at the moment? What do you miss the most?
- Are there any views you don't share with your fellow believers?
- For you, is there an only God or Goddess? Do you know His/Her name?
- Is deity (in your view) composed by a masculine and a feminine side?
- Are you mono- or polytheistic?
- If it doesn't make you uncomfortable, write down what you think happens to us after we die. It's interesting how many different answers you can get to this question, even among people who share the same religion.

Day 4: What Kind Of Witch Are You?

Most Witches I know are very open-minded people.

You will meet exceptions, just like everywhere, but they are usually non-judgmental and relatively unprejudiced people who tend to accept everyone as they are, no matter what their political, religious or gender identity choices are. That's why most of them are quick to dismiss labels, and many Witches frown upon society's efforts to classify and define them. So don't take the following paragraphs as a rigid, biology-class style classification of all existing Witches, but more as a loose explanation to help young Witches find their path. Because of its eclecticism, it is impossible to describe the magic community in a way which will fit all its members flawlessly, so I will ask my fellow Witches for a tiny bit of patience and understanding here.

Traditional Witchcraft can be compared to folk magic. It emphasizes the closeness to nature and doesn't need to follow strict rituals and ceremonies if the practitioner doesn't want to. It can be as simple as sending your intention to the Universe, or setting an altar in the middle of the forest by making a circle of stones, or as complex as casting a magic circle and creating a week-long spell with extremely rare ingredients. Traditional Witches can practice any religion and don't necessary believe in Wiccan dogmas, such as the *law of three* (see below).

Some Witches descend from a long line of Witches and healers, but many others don't. Most times, even for granddaughters of Witches the hereditary line was broken somewhere in the middle, due to social constraints and the obvious danger of being considered a Witch in certain communities. My aunt used to say she could foresee the future, enjoyed the occasional candle spell and loved to joke about herself being a Witch, but she never admitted such a thing in public, nor in serious conversation. Was she a true Witch? I think she was. But was she a Wiccan? Definitely not!

Some of my acquaintances have been able to expand their family trees and follow their ancestry line up to people condemned for Witchcraft centuries ago. And many people can remember their Witch ancestors, or themselves as Witches, during meditations and past life regressions. But even if you can't trace your ancestors, or know for certain none of them were Witches, it doesn't necessarily mean you can't become a Witch. It is believed that most people can develop their psychic abilities if they really want to and are open to learn new things. There is no reason why you couldn't be the first Witch in your family if you wish to.

Although Witches are not keen on adhering to strict labels, as I mentioned previously, most will agree on the differences between several Witch groups:

White Witches: white Witches only use magic to do good deeds. They believe that evil actions come back to the doer, and therefore never curse anyone or use magic to harm others. They don't cause damage deliberately and don't use magic to bend other people's will or change their preferences about something or someone (which means, for example, that they won't perform love spells to make other people fall in love against their will). They sometimes call themselves *good* Witches, probably because it helps them to be better accepted by society, as in opposition to the *evil* Witches most people know from folk tales (think about Snow White's and Rapunzel's stepmothers. Not the best role models out there, I guess).

Wiccan Witches: they follow the Wiccan religion, and adhere themselves to the rule of three: *"whatever you do, will be sent back to you threefold"*. If you do good deeds, good things will happen to you. If you harm others, you will be harmed in return, with triple force. Their philosophy is similar to the one of white Witches although their ways and their rituals might differ. White Witches, unlike Wiccans, don't harm others because they don't want to, and not necessarily because they are afraid of harm coming back their way (especially not *threefold*). They don't have specific rituals or deities. But in order to be a Wiccan you have to believe in Wiccan religion and its (few, but existing) rules. Many Wiccan Witches belong to closed groups, which are called covens.

A brief warning on joining a coven: always use your common sense if you decide to join a coven. There are many legit covens out there, but it is advisable to tread carefully in order to avoid being scammed. Beware if someone tries to force you to do things you don't want to do (of any kind), or suspect someone is trying to control your life, your finances or your friendships. I mentioned earlier that most Witches are nice people, but sadly, a few are not, and your priority should always be to stay safe. It's better to be a happy solitary Witch, than to belong to a coven full of people you don't like or trust.

Gray Witches: gray Witches use offensive magic when needed. They agree that all energy has a positive and a negative side, like the yin and yang, and nothing can be complete without both. There can't be light without dark or night without day, and nothing can't exist in the light without casting a shadow. Gray Witches can perform curses and hexes, but only if they have a good reason to do so. They don't believe bad energy will be sent back to them because of it, but they tend to be sparing with curses anyway. They rarely use *black* magic haphazardly. Imagine a criminal caused you or your family terrible damage. Would you be willing to sacrifice part of your personal energy in order to punish them with a curse? Do you think it would be forgivable to do so, in such an extreme case? Or would it be immoral to wish evil things upon others even if they wronged you? Do you think the Universe will punish them anyway, without your interference? These are delicate and personal questions we Witches must consider. Most traditional Witches are gray Witches, some of them leaning more towards the light and others towards the dark side of magic. You may be a white Witch *most of the time*, but one day you might cross paths with a really mean individual well worth making an exception.

Black Witches: first, a disclaimer: I don't know personally any real life *black* or *evil* Witches. They are supposed to cast malevolent spells and curses exclusively (with no altruistic goals whatsoever, just their own personal profit). Theoretically, they only use their magic skills to harm others. I don't think many such individuals exist, because most of us, humans, have a good and a bad side, do fair and unfair things, but it can be hard to be evil *all the time*. I suspect that even those who practice magic in order to harm others will use it to do good sometimes. A completely "dark" Witch might be the stereotype often found in fairy tales, which depicts a deeply disturbed individual, obsessed with attaining power, harming others and doing so just for fun. So, in my opinion, **true black Witches are rare, but there are just as many shades of gray Witches as people's opinions on what is fair and what is not.**

Some people name themselves *black* Witches, not because they want to be relentlessly evil, but because they adhere to Satanic or devil worshiping traditions. Interestingly enough, many traditional Witches don't even believe in the devil or hell as portrayed in the Bible: those are Christian concepts, and therefore irrelevant for non-Christian Witches.

Many religions like to label all Witches as Satanists and devil worshipers. But the actual percentage of devil-worshipping Witches is minute. You are probably more likely to meet Witches who worship Jesus, Gaia, Isis, the Virgin Mary, Ganesh, or even atheist Witches.

Most Witches like to identify themselves as Pagans or *heathens*, which simply means they don't practice any of the most widespread religions of the world (such as Christianism, Judaism, Islam, etc.). But you don't need to be a Pagan in order to be a Witch. Practicing Witchcraft —even sporadically— is enough.

Apart from the aforementioned types of Witches you will probably hear about *green Witches, hedge Witches, kitchen Witches*, etc. They might fall in one of the categories above (white, gray, Wiccan…). They share particular traits which help them define their path more easily, such as:

Kitchen Witches love to work with food and edible ingredients. Their craft tools are everyday utensils, such as kitchen knives and wooden spoons, pots and pans, herbs and condiments. They put their magic in the food they cook and the beverages they prepare, and share a love for the home and family life.

Hedge Witches are those who live on the border between our realm and the spirits' plane. They are supposed to communicate with those on the other side and can bring messages from one realm to the other. They can work with spirit animals and many times become healers. In many cultures they are represented by the shamans or healers of the village.

Green Witches are nature Witches, who work with the elements, the forests, the sea and the animals. They are well versed in herbal remedies and spells and share a deep love for the outdoors and all living creatures. They like to talk to the animals and trees, and many work with faeries and nature spirits. Some people have told me I am a green Witch because I love spending time in nature and I love taking care of plants and animals in need.

You will also find Celtic Witches, who share Celtic beliefs; there are also Druids, South American and Eurasian Shamans, Asatruans[4], Italian *streghe* and many other fascinating magical paths.

Finally, **Eclectic Witches** are quite common nowadays. They create their own path by mixing ideas and beliefs from

---

[4] *The Asatru worship Norse gods and spirits, such as Odin and Thor.*

different existing traditions. In this day and time, when people can easily connect and share information thanks to the development of telecommunications and the internet, it's not surprising that many Witches decide to create their unique path by combining several traditions: there is nothing wrong with that! Eclectic Witches are as well respected as the rest of members of the magic community.

What kind of Witch are you?

Maybe you don't know yet, but I hope today's exercise will help you start to figure it out. Your path may be twisting and winding. Some start as a kitchen Witch and later become a Druid. There is nothing wrong with that! We live, we learn, as the constantly evolving creatures we are. It's human nature, and part of the charm of being alive.

Today's task, to write in your journal:

1) Think about people you know:

- Do you know any Witches personally? If not, try to remember any celebrities, characters in books and TV shows, etc. How would you describe their path?

- What about other individuals you do know, but are not Witches? They can be anyone: family members, friends, co-workers or the cashier from the grocery store. Imagine they were Witches. What kind of Witches could they be?

2) Try to find out a bit more about yourself:

- Which, among the described philosophies, seems to make more sense for you right now?

- What do you know about your roots and heritage? Research what kind of Witchcraft was traditionally practiced where you live, or in your ancestors' countries. Try to find out about the names they gave themselves, their so-called superstitions, their rituals, etc. You might be delighted to find out your Russian or Sicilian great-grandparents had many traditions you can relate to or even recall.

Day 5: A Witch's Code of Ethics

There are very few rules to being a Witch. In my opinion, the only two rules all Witches should follow are:

1. *"Don't force your spiritual beliefs on others"*.
2. *"Respect other's beliefs and demand mutual respect from them"*.

That's it. This includes me and any teachers you will have in your life. Don't just believe and follow anything you read in this book (or anywhere, for that matter). Investigate, judge, and decide what is best for **you**.

This said, defining your personal code of ethics can't hurt: these are the ethical principles you will use to decide whether a certain practice is right or wrong.

1. Free will

The matter of free will is a much discussed one when talking about spells, and one Witches usually disagree on. Some people choose not to do any spells which might interfere with another person's free will, such as love spells. Such spells can go awry quickly, when the *bewitched* partner becomes obsessed, while the other part has already lost interest. You can cast a spell to help you find a new partner faster, or to make you more visible to potential partners, but I don't think you should use magic to force a certain person to love you.

On the other hand, there might cases when influencing someone's will, or stopping them from doing something harmful, could be for the highest good of all involved. (A brief disclaimer: I would only use this as a last resort after having had no success with all the worldly routes).

Some see nothing wrong in seeking magical revenge on someone who harmed or mistreated them or their loved ones. I would advise you not to do so, because —in my opinion— nothing good can be achieved from revenge, but the choice is ultimately yours. Curses can also be considered illegal in some countries. Some trust God, or Goddess, or a Higher Power, or Karma, to take care of such situations and put everyone in their place in the long run. Do bad things happen automatically to those who harm others? Or does the Universe need a little help to solve certain matters? Does the end justify the means? Maybe sometimes? You can also go a different route and send a healing or a *realization*[5] spell to the wrong-doer, so that they realize the harm they did, feel the guilt and never repeat it again. This can be the hardest thing to do, but I think it's very effective and free of the possible *rebound effect* of a curse.

Meditate on these matters and decide where your *right* and *wrong* stand. Also, consider that certain states or countries have laws which might punish people for hexing or even *threatening to hex* someone.

2. Types of spells

As we already discussed, love spells can be an apple of discord among Witches, but they are not the only source of disagreement. Think about spells related to health and healing or spells which could influence legal matters. *Of course, spells can never substitute the advice of a lawyer or a medical doctor*, but most Witches agree that attempting to send positive, healing energy to a sick or suffering person can't do any harm. But still, there are some people who would be furious if they discovered a Witch cast a healing spell for them (for example, people whose religious beliefs are against Witchcraft). Witches must respect other people's right to refuse their help and be left alone, even if it seems hard sometimes. It's a good habit to always ask for permission before doing anything.

3. Casting spells for others

Are you practicing magic just for yourself, or would you like to use magic to help others, too? Would you like to help your friends, your community, the whole planet Earth? (A great idea, actually). Do your beliefs allow you to do so?

---

[5] *Realization spell: a spell to help a wrong-doer become aware of the damage they caused to someone else.*

4. Taking money for your magic

First of all, it might not be legal to charge for spellwork where you live, or you might need to open a legal business of some sort in order to take payments or donations. This is the first thing you might have to check out if you want to become a professional Witch. Some people presuppose that Witches shouldn't be allowed to exchange their knowledge for money because the effectivity of their services is impossible to prove. Some cultures have superstitions related to Witches and money (e.g., some say that Witches should only take donations, or work for free, otherwise they could lose their *supernatural* abilities). Would you feel comfortable taking other people's money in exchange for a spell or a Tarot reading? For me, money is energy, and I see nothing wrong with exchanging one kind of energy for another. You may say you are exchanging hours of your life and this time should be fairly compensated. Some Witches like to barter, e.g., they will accept a haircut in exchange for a rune reading or a spell. You will also meet people who say true Witches should always help for free. But let's be real: learning Witchcraft can cost time and money. Witches, just like everyone else, have to buy books, take courses, get spell supplies, spend hours reading and practicing… even if all the materials were free, the time spent learning could have been used for something else. I think there is nothing wrong with people charging for their honest work and time. If someone comes to a Witch and asks for a divination reading, the Witch should have the right to put a price to their time and the services which are being freely requested by the customer, just like any other professional. It's the customer's choice to accept this price or reject it.

A note on psychic scams:

Sadly, scammers abound. Some unscrupulous people don't mind getting rich at the expense of desperate individuals. As a Witch, you don't want to become a victim, let alone be involved in such fraudulent activities. Psychic scammers give a bad name to honest Witches and readers, and they are the main reason people frown upon those who make a living out of their Witchcraft skills. Some people seek the help of a Witch when they have already tried everything. Despairing clients, who should be referred to a doctor or a psychologist instead, approach psychic services as a last resort. Genuine psychics keep emergency numbers handy for such cases, but there will always be fraudulent readers ready to take advantage of distressed clients. There is, for example, a well-known scam where a so-called reader tells their querent that they have been cursed, and then offers to remove said curse in exchange for an exorbitant sum of money. If the client is gullible enough, they will keep making up reasons for the client to come back, concocting stories about curses and bad luck which only *they* can stop. This kind of occurrences are sad and unfair, and give a bad reputation to honest Witches and readers.

Your task for today:

- Do you believe in karma, that is, are good and bad deeds eventually returned to the doer?
- Is it acceptable to use magic to change other people's will? What is your stance on love spells?
- Is it adequate to use magic to harm others? If so, in which cases?
- What is your opinion about people who charge for spells or divination services, such as Tarot, runes, etc.? Would you like to do such job for a living?
- If yes, or no, then why?

First Weekend: Cleansing and Scrying

1) Catching Up

Use the weekend to catch up with the days you had to skip because of life's obligations.

Re-read your journal's entries and complete them if you have any new ideas.

2) Illustrating

If you enjoy drawing, try to illustrate your journal entries. Drawing is a great form of meditation and will help you relax and remember the information you read during the week.

3) Cleansing And Manifesting Bath

Try to get at least half an hour just for yourself during this weekend, ideally on Sunday evening, as a corollary to your first magic journaling week.

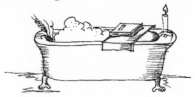

Get the bathroom for yourself, close the door and ask your family members or flat mates not to disturb you for a while. Take your journal and some candles/incense if you want to.

Open your journal and write today's date.

How do you feel today?

Fill the bathtub with water and light the candles and incense (please do so safely and never leave a burning candle unattended).

Get into the water and close your eyes. Quiet your thoughts, let them come and go like they were someone else's. Imagine your thoughts are just like the noise of the traffic: they are just there, but they don't affect you.

Now imagine what you would like to release from your life. Imagine how your worries and sorrows dissolve in the water. If you have a shower instead of a bath, imagine the running water cleansing your troubles and taking them down the drain.

Now try to say still until the surface of the water remains quiet. If you are showering, get dry and use the sink instead. Now disturb the surface of the water by sprinkling some drops with your hand or splashing on the surface of the water with your fingers. Look at the waves and shapes in the water attentively and try to see recognizable shapes, using your imagination. **This is known as scrying**, that is, watching the answers which come to mind when you look intently at a surface of water (it can also be done with mirrors, smoke, fire…).

- Think about your goals for next <u>week.</u>
- Think about your goals for next <u>year.</u>
- <u>What</u> would you like to achieve?

Try to visualize your desires as if they had already happened. Imagine yourself reflected in the moving water as your wishes come true. If you wish to pass an exam, try to visualize yourself in the waves of the water, as you come out of the exam happy and satisfied. If you are dreaming of finding a new home this year, see yourself cooking in your new kitchen or sunbathing in your new garden.

Before you go to bed, write about your cleansing ritual in your journal.

4) Collecting Supplies

If you go shopping this weekend, try to get some white candles and a safe candle holder (votive candles will do, but long tall candles are even better. Don't forget to get a candle holder: there is nothing more annoying than not being able to cast a spell because you have no way to keep your candles upright!).

CHAPTER 2:
A Witch's Box

This week we are going to put together a Witch's box. You will need very few tools for this task, and most supplies will be really easy to come by: half of them can probably be found in your home. Store-bought magical tools can be really nice to have, but making your own is a great and budget-friendly way to discover your preferences. Once you determine which tools you use the most, you can start shopping alternative fairs for the perfect Witch's utensils. To be honest, I enjoy my homemade versions more than any factory produced item, and crafting magical tools is one of my favorite pastimes.

You will also need a place to store your magical tools. Boxes with locks can be useful, especially if your flat mates tend to be too nosy, but a nice shoebox will do for a start. I just keep most of mine in a boring looking drawer, in my bedroom.

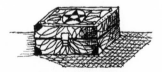

Day 6: Wands

You don't need a wand to be a Witch, and I am sure many Witches from the past didn't use one (if nothing else, for safety reasons, being such a well-known Witchcraft tool). They may have used just their pointed finger, a wooden spoon, or a twig picked up from the floor: something discreet, which could be passed off as a household tool or overlooked as an unimportant item.

But even if you don't absolutely need it, a wand is a great tool to focus and channel energy. Having a wand made by yourself and charged with your own energy will help you greatly in your Witchcraft practice. You can consider it your first step into the unknown, a symbol of your commitment to keep learning. You can use it as an extension of your hand, to help you attract and send condensed energy. For me, taking out my wand is part of the ritual, and it helps me focus. I can work without it, but when I have it, I know I am serious about what I am about to do. The whole ritual becomes more meaningful. When you first hold your wand, you might feel funny or childish, but really, you don't have to: I can assure you there are many serious adults on this planet who use wands surprisingly often.

Get a wand

Today, you will work on a new wand. Maybe you already have one: in that case, you can still bless it as explained at the end of this chapter, or you can make another one. There is nothing wrong with having more than one wand: I actually have three, all hand crafted by me, for different purposes. I also have a teeny-tiny one—not longer than a pencil!— which I carry in my suitcase when I travel. And sometimes I find a beautiful stick in the middle of the forest and use it as a makeshift tool to bless the trees or birds around me.

In order to carry out this exercise, go outside and try to find a fallen branch or a stick. If you can, visit a natural site (a forest, if you have access to one), or a bigger city park. Try to choose a fallen branch: this way, you will not damage any trees. If you decide to cut your wand from a tree, sit under the tree you have chosen and try to connect your thoughts with the energy of the tree. Tell the tree that you need a wand and try to hear its answer to your request. Is this tree willing to give you permission? Be mindful and don't cut any branches from privately owned trees, because the owner might be angry at you, no matter what the tree's opinion is! In case of doubt, pick only fallen branches from the floor. There might be a reason you came across them in your path.

If you have no way to get a twig, you can still do this exercise with a chopstick, a nice wooden pencil, a pretty hair stick, or a similarly shaped item from your household. Use your imagination!

The ideal length for a wand is supposed to be the same as your own forearm. But don't worry if you don't find one of the "perfect" length; sometimes, a tiny wand can work just as well as a full-length one. I also know of Witches who use magic staffs taller than themselves.

Decorating your wand:

Your wand is yours, and you can decorate it (or not) the way you prefer. Some ideas for you:

- Peel the tree bark (or leave it, for a rustic look),
- Engrave magic symbols on it (more about symbols on Chapter 5),
- Write a meaningful sentence or affirmation on it: a verse, a magic rule you follow, a prayer, a goal you mean to achieve with your magic, etc.
- Paint it,
- Add a crystal to the point,
- Cover it in twine or wool.

As you can see, the possibilities are endless. Just try: if you don't like the result, you can still undo it, or even make another one later.

Blessing your wand:

Pick up your wand with your dominant hand.

Close your eyes and take three deep breaths.

Try to relax all the muscles in your face, your shoulders and your arms.

When you feel ready, open your eyes.

Draw a clockwise circle around yourself with your wand. Imagine the point of your wand is drawing the outline of a circle of light, which becomes a sphere above your head and under your feet.

Lift the wand above your head, and imagine white, healing energy descending from the sky. It can be like a white, purple or golden lightning. See how the light enters your wand through the point and charges it with positive energy.

Then look at the wand and repeat the following words. If you don't identify with them, you can also write your own. Intention matters more than the actual words you use.

> *"I name you my wand,*
> *To serve me and assist me in my craft,*
> *May we work successfully together,*
> *May you help me achieve my goals,*
> *May you channel my magic,*
> *And serve me well as long as our partnership lasts.*
> *As I say it, it is done.*
> *It is done, it is done, it is done."*

Now point the wand at your own head and imagine the healing energy spreading from your head to the rest of your body. Close your eyes and feel the light bathing you and purifying you. See the light going out through the tips of your toes and disappearing slowly into the earth. Feel the connection with your wand and thank it when the energy flow stops.

You will know when it is time to end the ritual. Open the circle you drew by drawing another, anticlockwise circle with the tip of your wand, starting at the same point where you finished.

Take a few deep breaths and drink a glass of water before you go on with your day.

Day 7: The Elements

The four elements, as understood by most Witches, are the building blocks of everything around us. They should not be mistaken with the chemical elements from the periodical table. The magical elements are not an exact science, but a symbolic way to classify things in our environment. This means that the element of fire, for example, doesn't have to refer to a flame, but it can comprise many other related concepts or objects, such as, for example: passion, rage, the summer, a red stone, etc.

Different cultures have described the elements in different ways, and some use five instead of four elements, but the most widespread division in Western culture is the following:

Air: represented by the air we breathe and the color yellow, and related to thoughts and mental processes. For example, a conversation or an idea would belong to the Element of Air.

Earth: represented by stones and crystals, dirt, plants and trees, and the color green, and related to material wealth, health and physical/tangible things. For example, money or a plot of land would belong to the element of Earth.

Fire: represented by fire itself and the color red. It is related to the masculine, passion, creativity, and phallic shapes. Some examples might be: being passionate about something, or having an argument with someone.

Water: represented by bodies of water and vessel shapes (such as a cup or a bowl). Related to the feminine (the womb of the Goddess, the Great Mother), to feelings and nurturing others, and the color blue.

AIR   EARTH   WATER   FIRE

Some add a Fifth Element: Spirit, or ether, the invisible force which makes everything alive and which could also be interpreted as energy or magic.

These elements can also be found in the traditional suits of a Tarot deck:

- Swords - Air
- Pentacles or Discs - Earth
- Wands or Rods - Fire
- Cups or Chalices - Water

And in the four seasons of the year:

- Air - Winter
- Earth - Spring
- Fire - Summer
- Water - Autumn / Fall

And the four cardinal points:

- Air - North
- Earth - East
- Fire - South
- Water - West

There are many other things you can relate to the four Elements, for example, the signs of Western Astrology, Gods and Goddesses, Crystals, etc.

If you are of Asian (especially Chinese) descent or feel identified with Asian culture, you might prefer to use the Five Elements as known in Traditional Chinese Medicine and Feng Shui: Earth, Water, Wood, Fire and Metal. Feel free to use this variation of the elements if they are more meaningful to you because of your heritage or your personal beliefs.

Today's task:

Find a representation of each of the (4 or 5) elements. You can find them in your own home or garden, or get them outside. Some examples:

- Air: feathers, incense, something yellow.
- Earth: a bowl of dirt, salt, stones, crystals.
- Water: seashells, a cup of water, blue things.
- Fire: candles, something red.

Put on a table all the things you found and sort them by the element they belong to. Find the North direction with a compass, or look at the position of the Sun from your window (for orientation, the Sun rises in the East and sets in the West). Arrange your elemental groups like this:

- Air - North
- Earth - East
- Fire - South
- Water - West

Hold each of the objects separately and try to feel the energy of each different Element in your hands. Imagine how it spreads all over your body. Do you sense the same when you hold the stone and the glass of water?

Write about the four elements in your journal, noting a few examples of each, and draw the symbol for each element for practice.

Day 8: Ritual Knives

Some Witches like to own special knives, which they reserve for their craft only. The most common types are called *athames* and *bolines.*

Athame (left) and boline (right).

In the Wiccan tradition the athame is an important ritual tool. Athames are ceremonial knives, and they are usually blunt and double edged. Most of the times they have a black handle. They are never used to cut anything, just to direct energies or to draw boundaries (in the air or on the earth). They represent the divine masculine and the element of air.

Athames are often used in rituals, such as the depiction of the Great Rite (a representation of the union between masculine energy (the knife) and feminine energy (the vessel)). But even if you are Wiccan, you don't need to have an athame. Some state laws may forbid you to own one, depending on its shape and the material it is made of. You can still use a simple butter knife or a wooden knife for your magic. I have actually seen some lovely handcrafted, wooden athames. Some people use a feather instead of an athame, as it belongs to the element of air. I just use my index finger, or my wand, but I am not a Wiccan anyway.

Bolines, on the other hand, are sharp and usually have a white handle. They are used for actual cutting and carving.

Some people allege that athames and bolines became popular because of Gerald Gardner, aka the father of modern Witchcraft, who spent many years in Malaysia, where he developed a great appreciation for the ritual knives used by the natives (he actually published a book named *Keris and other Malay weapons,* in 1936[6]). For these reasons, athames *might* be a relatively new addition to Witches' tools, and some traditional Witches avoid them, considering it a newer addition to the craft.

I would like to add that I have never owned an athame

---

[6] *Wikipedia, Gerald Gardner (Wiccan), Online, seen on:*
https://en.wikipedia.org/wiki/Gerald_Gardner_(Wiccan) *(2017).*

nor a boline, because I don't feel comfortable using knives as ritual or spell tools: I consider knives, ritual or not, a potential weapon, and this is why I prefer not to have one of them in my home. If I need to cut anything, the tools already present in my kitchen are more than enough. But I am aware that no book on Witchcraft would be complete without at least acknowledging the existence of athames and bolines, which are well loved and used by many successful Witches, especially in the Wiccan and Neopagan traditions.

Today's assignment:

For this assignment, search for a kitchen knife, a stainless steel skewer, a chopstick, or even a toothpick from your kitchen. I wouldn't go out and shop for a "true" athame on the first day: there will be plenty of time for that later. If you still want to buy one, check for athames, bolines and similar tools online, or at local garage sales and second-hand shops. For today, let's just use something you already have at home, to see what it feels like to work with ceremonial knives.

This is a similar exercise to the one we performed with the wand:

Practice 1: The Athame

- Close your eyes and take three deep breaths.
- Draw a clockwise circle around yourself, using your athame. Imagine its point is drawing the contour of a circle of light, which becomes a sphere above your head and under your feet.
- Lift your arm and imagine your athame is like an antenna which attracts and draws pure energy from the sky. Keep your arm up and feel the energy as it flows through you and exits through your toes, drawing all negativity out of your body and substituting it with unconditional love and acceptance.
- Take as much time as you desire.

- When you feel ready, close the circle.

Practice 2: the Boline

For this exercise, you will need:

- A candle (long, white candles are the best)
- A relatively sharp object, which will be used to carve a few words on the candle. I have had success with knitting needles, crochet hooks and other sewing tools. This will be our boline.
- A kitchen knife and a piece of rope

Note: I don't like using objects which are too sharp because I tend to be clumsy and I'm not interested in hurting my fingers in the process...

1. Think about a goal you would like to achieve right now. Let's imagine goal were to get a job. Try to reduce your wish to one brief word: in this case, JOB. If the word is long, you can shorten it.
2. Using your carving tool, carefully carve this word on the body of the candle.
3. Mark three horizontal lines on the candle, at different heights.
4. Put the candle on a safe candle holder, on a stable, non-flammable surface away from curtains and winds currents.
5. Now imagine the three steps you would have to take in order to achieve your goal. For example:
   a. Beginning situation: *right now I am jobless.*
   b. Action to take: *I apply for my dream job.*
   c. Result: *I am offered the job I wanted.*
6. Using your makeshift boline, cut a piece of rope.
7. Now make three knots on the rope. Each one will be one of the steps to take. Name each step aloud while you do it.
8. Light the candle and watch it burn. When the flame reaches the first line you drew, say: *"I used to be jobless, that's now in the past"*. Untie the first

knot and cut and discard that piece of rope. Use your boline to cut it.

9. When it reaches the second line, say: *"I am working to find a better job"*. Then untie the second knot and cut off the second third of rope.

10. Finally, when the flame reaches the third line, say: *"Thank you for this job I am being offered. Thank you, thank you, thank you"*.

11. *You can now snuff the candle.*

12. Keep the last piece of rope always with you until your wish comes true. You should soon see signs of change.

Important note: *some countries consider the possession of athames or bolines to be illegal. Please check out the minimum age and other requirements if you decide to buy one. Please exercise caution when working with candles and sharp objects and keep them out of the reach of children and pets. You can still be a great Witch without a ceremonial knife. Or without most "must-haves", for that matter.*

Day 9: Divination tools

Divination is an art practiced by many Witches, and one of the best-known magical practices nowadays. You don't have to be a Witch to use divination tools, but the use of ritual and the heightened intuition distinctive of Witches can definitely help you get better readings.

Today we will focus on **pendulums**, because they are the easiest divination tool you can create at home. Divination is a great addition at the end of a meditation session (more on meditation in the next Chapter). No matter what urban legends say, you don't need any attention numbing procedures or dangerous substances to your rituals: stay away from them, because they will just make you confused and affect your attention negatively. You need to keep a clear head in order to read your divination tools properly.

Meditation is much safer, and it will help you be calm and focused, and achieve better results.

Today: working with a pendulum.

Creating your pendulum:

A pendulum is one of the easiest divination tools you can make. You just need a bead, coin or stone hung from a piece of string or a thin necklace. If you own, for example, a silver chain and a pendant or a ring, this will work perfectly as a pendulum. There is no need to buy a factory-made pendulum in order to get started out.

Using a pendulum:

1. In order to use a pendulum just take a deep breath and extend your arm horizontally, at arm level. Let the pendulum swing freely. Breathe normally and try to relax your arm as much as possible.

2. First, you will have to calibrate your pendulum. Think about a *yes/no* question you know the answer for, such as: *"is my name Mary? / Am I wearing glasses?"* Breathe normally and observe the movement of the pendulum until it becomes stable. It might move backwards and forwards, sideways, or roll clockwise or anticlockwise. Whatever it does, it is fine. Pendulums respond differently to different people. Even the same pendulum can work differently during your next session, so it's good to ask it a couple test questions (calibrate it) each time before you start asking it more important questions.

3. Once you have found out which movement stands for *yes* and which one stands for *no*, you can start asking some divination questions. I recommend you to start out with trivial questions you will find out about soon, such as: *will my mother call this evening? Will John come home before 5:00PM?* Write down your answers in your journal and check them later to see your accuracy rate. Don't worry if it doesn't work out at first, just keep trying. The key is to keep your arm completely relaxed so that your own

expectations don't influence the answer. As you progress, you may start getting better results. But don't worry if you discover you are not good with pendulums, there are still many other alternative divination techniques you can try.

How to hold a pendulum between your thumb and index fingers.

Other methods of divination you can try:

Runes: you will need 24 stones, pebbles or pieces of wood of similar size and shape. If you live near a river or a beach, you will have no problems finding them. Draw a rune on each pebble and put them in a little bag. In Chapter 8 you will find a list of Norse runes, their meanings and their depiction.

You can use your runes to answer questions. Simply pick one to three pebbles from the bag and find their meaning on the list. Write down your readings in your journal and try to create a story out of the keywords.

A quick example of how you can use your runes:

Question: *"how can I find out about my true vocation?"*

Procedure: I picked from the bag the runes Ansuz and Raido. I check out their meanings:

- Ansuz: "wisdom". Related to Odin. Learning, wisdom, divine guidance.
- Raido: "wheel". Journey, traveling, movement, messages, a good time to start.

Answer: *"the answer will be revealed to you while traveling".*

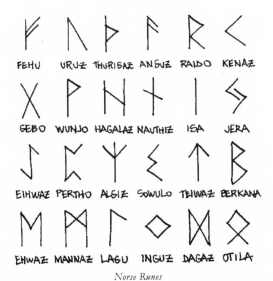

Norse Runes

Divination cards: Tarot, oracle cards, Lenormand, Kipper, Etteila: among these, my hands-down favorite is Tarot, although I practice some others occasionally. I got my first deck many years ago: it was made of cheap cutout cards and it came for free with a teen magazine. I still remember one of my first readings, which happened to fulfill itself. I was so impressed by that reading that I decided I had to learn to read Tarot properly (that was a bit harder in the pre-internet era!). It is beyond the scope of this book to teach you Tarot to a professional level, but you can start with the handy keyword list which can be found in the last pages. If you realize Tarot might be for you, I encourage you to do some research of your own: Tarot can offer you extremely deep and meaningful answers to your questions. Some like to use it as a reflection and introspection tool. I must warn you, though, that the study of Tarot can last for a lifetime: there are always new layers of meaning and symbolism you will be able to learn and add to your readings. If you can't afford a Tarot deck at this point, but you still want to try, you can easily start with a deck of conventional cards, making the following substitutions:

> Swords - Spades
> Pentacles - Diamonds
> Wands - Clubs
> Cups - Hearts

The only difference is that playing cards have no Major Arcana (so, there is no Fool, Moon, Death, etc.). But you will be able to learn the meanings for the cards from the ace to the King of each suit, which is already very useful.

You can also try to get a second-hand deck from a buy-and-sell website. I recommend you to start with the **Rider-Waite-Smith** deck or one of its modernized versions.

Another possibility is to make your own deck by sketching it on 78 pieces of construction paper (or make just the Major Arcana for a start).

If you already practice other forms of divination, you can use today's practice to sit down with a book to deepen your knowledge or do a reading or two on a matter of your interest.

Day 10: Creating An Altar

There are many kinds of altars, and even the understanding of what an altar is varies from Witch to Witch. Most will agree that an altar is a place where you can practice your magic. If you are religious, you will also use your altar as a place of worship for your deities. If you live alone, or don't mind other people in your house knowing about your magic practices, you will be able to keep your altar in a visible place in your home. Most Witches prefer to have their altar indoors, in a discreet spot, such as a bedroom dresser, or even in a closet, or in a drawer they can just open and close when needed. Others keep wonderful outdoor altars, which range from simple circles of rocks to elaborated garden designs. You can work without an altar, too, or set it up only when you need it (on your kitchen table, for example), then put your tools back into their box after using them. This can be a good option if you have playful pets or young children at home.

A simple altar set-up

Traditionally, altars should be set up facing north. You can forego this condition if you have space constrictions.

Today we will arrange an altar with the tools you have been collecting during the last days. You will need:

- *An altar cloth:* an altar cloth helps you delimitate the space of your altar. You can use a piece of fabric, a shawl or even a neat napkin. Put it on a dresser or a small table.
- *The representation of the four elements:* a few days ago your task was to find several items which represented the four elements. Put them on your altar, facing the corresponding direction. The most common are:
    - *A cup of water,* to represent water and the divine feminine.
    - *A candle,* used for spells and as a representation of the element of fire.

- ○ *Your athame, if you have one*, to represent the divine masculine, the element of air, and to draw your magic circle,
- ○ *A bowl of salt or a crystal*, to represent the element of earth.

- Finally, you can place <u>your wand</u> on the altar, too. It can also substitute the candle as the element of fire.

Some Witches add the following to their altars:

- **A cauldron:** you can brew your teas in ordinary kitchen pots. An iron caldron has a place in a Witch's home, though, especially when you need a safe place to burn a piece of paper, for example, when doing banishing spells, and for spells which require cooking and brewing certain ingredients.

- **A pentacle:** the pentacle is a symbol of Witchcraft, Paganism, and the five elements (the four elements, plus *Spirit* or *ether*). Pentacles are considered sacred by many Witches and most have one on their altar, just like Christians keep a cross over their beds or wear one in a chain. Pentacles are thought by some to be evil or to be related to Satanism, but this is definitely not true. Some Satanic cults choose to use *inverted* crosses and *inverted* pentacles. They <u>invert them</u> in order to imply <u>the opposite</u> of their original meaning. You can draw a pentacle on a round piece of wood or cardboard, or on a piece of fabric, and use it as the central piece of your altar. Use it later to place the ingredients of your spells.

- ***Figures or paintings of their deities.*** Celtic Witches may honor Brigid, the Asatru might worship Odin, etc. Some Witches have a matron Goddess, or a God and a Goddess they revere as a representation of the masculine and feminine forces which form our Universe. Hekate is considered the protector Goddess of all Witches.

Once you have finished, you can leave your altar where it is, or put everything back in a safe, discreet place. If you leave it out, don't forget to dust it regularly. **You can also add seasonal decorations to your altar,** such as pumpkins for fall, mistletoe for winter, etc. Decorate your altar the way you want, respect other people's beliefs and hopefully they will respect yours, too.

A tiny portable altar, which can fit in a candy tin.

Second Weekend: Hugging Trees

1) Catch Up

This weekend take the necessary time to catch up with the week's assignments.

If you haven't managed to get a wand, or candles, or to get and test a divination tool, now it's the time to do it.

Update your journal and record last week's practices. Write what you did, what you expected, the results and how you felt afterwards. Think about the things you liked and the things you might want to change the next time.

2) Have A Walk: The Plants Around You

Have a walk around your neighborhood. If possible, find a park or a place with tall trees. Look around you. Pay attention to the other living beings around you. Try to find a calm spot with as much vegetation as possible.

Stand under the biggest tree you can find and try to feel its energy. Hug it and close your eyes. Try to connect with the tree. Imagine the sap flowing inside it. Visualize all the things this tree has seen since it germinated from a tiny seed. Was there a city around it when it was just a sapling? Was the forest bigger, deeper, wider, back then? Hear what this tree would tell you if it could. It may actually tell you something.

When you get back, write about your experience in your journal.

3) Go Shopping Or Find The Following At Home:

- If you didn't get them last week, now it's time to get some candles. Get at least a few white candles. You can also buy a couple of red, green or yellow candles.

- If you didn't get it last week, find or make a candle holder. If you are crafty, you could make one out of modeling clay.

- Herbs: if you have absolutely no spices in your kitchen, this weekend you may want to add a few to your grocery shopping list. Consider buying some garlic, bay leaves and cinnamon. Don't worry, even if you end up doing no spellwork, you can still use them for cooking.

4) Take A Cleansing Bath

Follow last week's instructions and find at least twenty minutes for yourself to have a peaceful shower or a bath. Imagine the water taking away all your sorrows and worries and see them disappear with the dirty water as it goes down the drain.

CHAPTER 3:
Magic Ingredients

Soon you will realize that you need very few ingredients to cast a spell. You can even cast spells in your head, using visualization or working in the astral plane[7]. Some Witches like to use intricate spells full of rare ingredients, while others forego most of them and are successful just the same. When you are starting, assigning a meaning to each ingredient will help you state your intentions clearly, and the task of casting a spell will become faster, easier and more effective. Don't worry, most of what we are going to use is very inexpensive and easy to find.

Day 11: Candle Magic

Candles are such a versatile magic tool that some Witches choose to do candle magic exclusively. They are discreet (they can be easily disguised as decorations), inexpensive and seemingly quite effective.

Candle colors: the only candle color you will ever need is white, because it can substitute all the rest. Witches from the past didn't have as many color choices as we have now, so don't worry if your budget is tight, just get a few white, universal candles.

---

[7] *Some Witches affirm they can visit the astral world at will, that is, they are able to visit places with only the inmaterial part of their beings. Such places can be on this world or other ethereal, dream-like locations. They can create their altar and find spell ingredients while in the astral plane. Most of us, however, only enter the astral world occasionally and by chance —if at all—, for example while sleeping or when in deep meditation. It is said many of us had this ability as children, and lost it later in life as we reached adulthood.*

Still, many Witches enjoy working with colored candles, because they can add an extra layer of meaning to spells. When purchasing or making colored candles, follow the following guidelines:

- <u>Money and health spells:</u> green, yellow, golden
- <u>Love spells:</u> red, pink
- <u>Banishing spells</u>: black

Today's task:
We are going to cast a small candle spell.

1. Think about something you would like to attract or banish into your life. In my example, I will make a spell to manifest the necessary money to pay my rent this month.
2. Take a white or correspondingly colored candle and put it in a safe candle holder. For my money spell, I will use a green candle.
3. With an old ball-pen or another sharp object (a boline, if you have one), carve one or two words which best summarize the goal of your spell. For my example, I would carve: *rent money*, or *RM*.
4. Place a sewing pin at approximately medium height if you are working with tall candles. If you don't have any sewing pins, use a push pin or simply draw or carve a line around the candle.
5. Now write your spell. Be as specific as you can. You can use the text below and substitute the text in brackets so that it better suits your intentions:

[Five-hundred dollars], I manifest.
Before the end of this month,
Whatever happens, will be for the best,
And I will [keep this cozy home].
[Money] comes swiftly to me,
This spell has no ill effects
on me or the people around me,
My highest good it will serve.

So it is, so it is, so it is.

6. Hold your wand up and imagine how it gathers energy, like a current of electricity coming down from the sky and into your wand.

7. When you feel like there is enough energy, read your spell three times, and after the third time, light the candle.

8. Finally, point at the candle with your wand (you don't have to actually touch the candle, just point at it), and imagine the energy flowing from your wand and imbuing the candle.

9. Let the candle burn until it reaches the pin or the mark. Once it reaches that point, your spell is completed. (Extra points if the pin falls off!). You can dispose of the candle or keep it on your altar for as long as you like, or until your wish is granted.

Safety warning: when working with candles please be careful and never leave a candle unattended or near fabric items such as curtains or tablecloths. If you must leave the room or can't stay next to your burning candle just put it off and light it again later, when you come back.

How to blow out a candle: some Witches consider that blowing a candle is disrespectful to the element of air. I do not abide by this rule, but you can choose to follow it if you want. In that case, use a candle snuffer or a metallic spoon to put it off (beware, snuffing tools can become hot and their surface might become scorched). If you have no snuffer, you can also ask the element of air for permission before blowing out your candle.

How to resume a candle spell: sometimes you won't have enough time to wait for a candle to extinguish itself. If you must leave the room, or go to sleep, it is safest to blow out the candle and resume your spell when you are back and have enough time to keep it under surveillance. **In order to resume your spell, read the text three times and relight**

the candle. You can pause a spell as many times as you need until the candle is completely consumed.

Once the candle has completely melted, read your spell for a final time and say:

It is done, it is done, it is done.

This expression, repeated three times, is often used as a strong affirmation which signs the successful end of a spell. Some Witches prefer to use the words ***"so mote it be"***, which mean approximately the same.

Once the molten wax has solidified, it is safe to dispose of the remains of the candle, if there are any.

Day 12: Herbs

Herbs can be used for many purposes in Witchcraft. Some of them are:

- ***Teas and beverages:*** some edible herbs are safe to be drank as teas and decoctions. Some can have healing properties, and experienced herbalists know a herb for almost each ailment. Peppermint, chamomile and ginger are good examples of herbs which lend themselves to be used in teas.
- ***Potions and filters:*** these are herbal decoctions are not meant to be drank, but sprinkled, poured on something or kept in bottles, depending on the spell. They may contain non-edible ingredients. They should never be ingested.
- ***Baths:*** you can add herbs to your bath water to infuse it with their powers.
- ***Herbal pouches:*** herbal pouches are bags full of dried herbs, which are worn or kept as talismans, for example, to attract good fortune

or keep bad influences at bay.

- **_Burning herbs_**: some spells call for herb burning. For this kind of spell it is useful to have a cast iron cauldron or a fire safe container where you can do so.

Today's assignment:

Today I would like you to go outside and look closely at the plants which grow near you. I want you to pay special attention to the weeds, those nobody looks at, the ones which grow next to the roads, in abandoned plots of land or in forest clearings. Many of them are highly useful for Witches, and they are freely available. Some of the most common wild herbs you can find in the vicinity of populated places are:

- **_Plantain:_** it can be used as a protection amulet or a divination aid.
- **_Yarrow:_** protects against negativity, sharpens the intuition and is used in healing spells.
- **_Dandelion:_** if you find a dandelion seed head you can make a wish before blowing it. When you blow it, you will send your message to the Universe. Yellow dandelion flowers can be used to attract positive energy and in money spells.
- **_Nettle_** (careful, it stings!): stinging nettle is a strong protective herb, which can also be used to reflect and send back negativity to someone who is doing you harm or wishing you bad. You can carry it in a pouch or make a broom of nettles (use paper as a handle to protect your hands), and sweep the negativity out of your

house and back to the sender.

- *Clover:* four-leaved clovers are a worldwide symbol of good luck, but they can be hard to come by. Ordinary three-leaved clover can be used instead for love and money spells, or whenever seeking for general good luck. It is said fairies love clover plants, and they seemingly love to gather in clover patches at night. Sow clover in your garden in order to make your local *faeries* happy.

Other herbs you can find in your own home:

- *Love spells*: rose petals (fresh or dried), vanilla, cinnamon, lavender flowers.
- *Protection spells:* garlic, cumin, rosemary.
- *Money spells:* bay leaves, thyme, ginger
- *Wish granting and multipurpose spells:* bay leaves, rosemary.

Today, try to find at least three different herbs from the list and stick them in your journal. Check in your pantry or go for a walk. If you find your herbs outside, make an effort to find out their name and properties, and write them next to the leaves and flowers you collected. For this, you will probably have to do some research: use the internet, join an herbalism forum or ask local people. There are many online groups where people help each other identify herbs. You can also download several phone apps which allow you to recognize a plant just using your phone camera.

Please exercise caution when collecting herbs, because some can be poisonous, stingy or trigger allergies. Never eat or prepare a tea from an herb if you are not sure it was identified properly, because there are several plants with poisonous lookalikes (for example, poison hemlock is very similar to yarrow, while wild garlic looks almost the same as crow's poison, and the lookalikes can be deadly).

If, for any reason, you can't collect any real herbs, you can just draw them in your notebook instead.

This exercise will help you to start paying attention to the herbs which are already growing around you. If you enjoy it, consider making your own herbarium at home. Later on, you might even want to become an herbalist Witch. If so, find a good course or an experienced mentor to guide you and show you how to identify, collect and prepare the different herbs which grow in your surroundings.

If you are going to use herbs internally (e.g., in teas or salads), always buy them from a reputable source, unless you are a very confident collector. Follow the advice of a qualified herbalist when working with any herbs you don't know. Even edible herbs can be poisonous, depending on the dose, so please exert caution and, when in doubt, don't eat them. Remember that many drugs are made from plants, and certain teas and spices could interfere with medications. In case of doubt, always ask your doctor first.

Day 13: Crystals and Chakras

Crystals are a great magic tool which can be used for spells, meditation and manifestation. All Witches should possess at least a basic knowledge of crystals and their possible benefits. In today's chapter, we will study **crystals and their relationship with our chakras**.

On acquiring your first crystals

If you don't have any crystals yet, don't just run out to buy a bunch of specimens because of this book. Look around yourself: you might realize that you already own a few crystals, maybe right in front of you, in your engagement ring.

When purchasing crystals, **try to find ethically mined pieces**, because crystal mining can be very detrimental for our planet. You want to get crystals mined by fairly paid adults working with proper protection and using low impact extraction methods. Ethical vendors will usually state the origin of their pieces in their listings. Otherwise, you can always ask.

Small, tumbled stones, are a good place to start: they are inexpensive and easy to find. Ideally get yourself a *chakra set*, that is, one crystal of a different color for each of the seven chakras. Having crystals in seven different colors can prove very versatile in the long run.

Some crystals are more expensive than others, but **effectivity is not directly proportional to price**. Prices depend on demand and supply, are some low-cost crystals, like selenite, can yield great results and prove themselves very cost-effective.

Crystal properties and classification

Different crystals have different energies, but don't expect to find exactly the same descriptions in each crystal book you read. Sometimes, the classification of their properties can be a bit loose. One summer, while visiting an alternative fair, each of the stalls I checked out had a slightly different list of properties for amethyst. None of them was wrong: the same crystal can have dozens of uses.

When you meet a certain type of crystal for the first time, you can try to guess its possible uses just by looking at the color.

Each color is associated to a different chakra (an energy center located at a certain area of the body; more about chakras later), which is useful when using crystals to aid with spells. You can even find alternative practitioners who work with *crystal healing*, or combine crystals with other modalities.

According to their color, we can classify crystals as

follows:

Red crystals:
- **Carnelian,** garnet, topaz.
- Motivation, passion, passionate love, courage, blood, the masculine, determination and warmth.
- *Root chakra.*

Pink crystals:
- *Rose quartz.*
- Used against stress, promote friendship, romantic love, Platonic love, and self-love.
- *Heart chakra.*

Orange crystals:
- **Carnelian.**
- Positive energy, optimism, creativity.
- *Sacral chakra.*

Yellow and golden crystals:
- **Citrine,** amber (not a crystal, but used in magic, too), tiger's eye.
- Success, wealth, optimism, happiness, protection.
- *Solar plexus chakra.*

Green crystals:
- Peridot, aventurine, malachite, jade.
- Health, rest, relaxation, truth, love.
- *Heart chakra.*

Blue crystals:
- **Angelite,** blue lace agate.
- Communication, peace, angelic influences.

- *Throat chakra.*

Indigo/Dark blue crystals:
- **Sodalite,** lapis lazuli.
- Awareness, vision, deep understanding.
- *Third eye chakra.*

Purple crystals:
- **Amethyst.**
- Spiritual growth, intuition, higher self, the feminine, magic and mysterious matters.
- *Crown chakra.*

Black and dark gray crystals:
- **Black obsidian**, black tourmaline, jet, apache tears, smoky quartz.
- Mostly protective, often very strong energies.

White or transparent crystals:
- **Clear quartz**, calcite
- Used for mental clarity, peace and purity.

Location of the main chakras

The concept of chakras comes from Eastern cultures,

but it's widely used nowadays all over the world, especially by the New Age movement. **Chakras can be described as wheels of light or spinning spirals of energy**, located over certain areas of the body. When the body is healthy, chakras are supposed to spin harmoniously. When we are ill or distressed, chakras are said to start spinning slowly or even stop completely (you have probably heard about "blocked" or "closed" chakras). Sometimes, when we use a part of our body excessively, chakras may start spinning too fast, becoming exhausted in the long run (this is known as an "overactive" or "overly open" chakra). There are more than one hundred chakras, but the most widely used and known are the following seven:

1. ***Root chakra.*** Base of the spine. Red.
2. ***Sacral chakra.*** Lower abdomen. Orange.
3. ***Solar plexus chakra.*** Middle of the abdomen. Yellow.
4. ***Heart chakra.*** Heart area. Green (sometimes related to pink, too).
5. ***Throat chakra.*** Neck area. Blue.
6. ***Third eye chakra.*** Between the eyebrows. Indigo.
7. ***Crown chakra.*** Top of the head. Purple.

How to use a crystal chakra set:

1. Meditating with crystals

A great way to use your crystals is to meditate with them.

A. Pick one crystal out of your collection, with your eyes closed. This will be the focus of your meditation for that day. For example, if you pick a red crystal, sit down in a comfortable position, while holding it in your hands, and find ways to nurture the energy of your root chakra, that is, your personal power, your primal instincts, etc.

B. Lie down on your bed or a comfortable mat. Align your crystals next to you, in a way you can easily reach them when you extend your hand. Starting with the lowest chakra (the root chakra), put a red crystal on it and imagine how the energy of this chakra becomes clean, and the chakra starts to spin beautifully, not too fast and not too slow. Afterwards do the same with the rest of your chakras. Once you have placed all the crystals on the right points, close your eyes and imagine how your body is now becoming balanced and healthy. With your mind's eye, see all your chakras spinning nicely and shining with a bright light, each one of a different color.

2. Manifestation

When writing a spell or trying to manifest a wish, set on your altar the crystals which agree with your intention, or wear them on yourself (a pocket is fine). For example:

- When manifesting money or business success, place **citrine** on your altar,
- When trying to deepen your intuition or your understanding of a certain matter, use an amethyst,
- When trying to attract love or self-love, you can carry a **rose quartz** in your pocket.

For more information about cleaning the energy of your crystals when they become saturated, refer to Chapter 5 (cleansing methods).

Day 14: Tarot card spells

Today we are going to do a simple Tarot card or runes spell. In order to do this, you will need one of the following:

a) A Tarot deck, if you own one, or a set of runes

(they will work, whether bought or homemade).

b) A deck of playing cards.

c) If you have none of that, you can print[8] or draw the cards you need.

First, try to reflect about the goal of your spell. In my example, I will create a spell to increase my intuition. You can decide to do a different spell, using the same technique.

Look at the list of card meanings and choose the one which expresses your wish best. Some examples:

- In order to strengthen my intuition, I'd choose **The High Priestess**.

- If I wished to become a mother or to nurture my creativity, I'll pick **The Empress.**

- In order to attract love, use **The Lovers** and/or the **Two of Cups.**

- In order to attract money, choose the **Ace of Pentacles** or the **10 of pentacles.**

- In order to attract happiness, choose **The Sun,**

- In order to attract success, choose the **Six of Wands.**

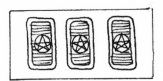

---

[8] *You should be able to find some Public Domain Tarot decks on the internet, available for personal use, which you will be able to print at home and use for the exercises in this book. Public Domain decks are mostly reproductions of XVIII Century Marseille decks, which were created more than 200 years ago. The Major Arcana in these decks are similar to the RWS system, although the Minor Arcana cards are usually not illustrated (this is what we call "pip cards").*

Now write the text of your spell. The best spells are supposed to rhyme, but don't worry if you are no Shakespeare. I'm not either, but I do my best: it's your spell, just do it your way.

Before you use a spell written by someone else, copy it in your journal or on a piece of paper and change the parts you need.

A *spell to enhance your intuition*

(This spell is meant to be used together with the High Priestess card from any Tarot deck).

With this spell
my intuition becomes deeper,
my understanding wider,
my knowledge vaster,
and as I get stronger,
so do my magic powers.

Oh, High Priestess,
lift the veil for me,
make my magic powerful,
with each day that I live.

And so it is, so it is, so it is.

Once the text of the spell is ready, wait for a moment when you know you won't be disturbed. Set your altar and take a few deep breaths. Meditate for a short time if you can.

Before you start casting the spell, have the following items within reach:

- Wand (and your athame, if you use one),
- Tarot deck or runes,
- Journal and written spell.

How to proceed:

- Place the journal, open by the page where your spell is written, in the middle of your altar.
- Cast a magic circle with your wand or athame.
- Hold your wand with one hand (dominant/writing hand) and the chosen Tarot card with the other one (receptive hand).
- Read the spell three times.
- Once you finish, touch the card with the tip of your wand.
- Place the Tarot card in the middle of your altar.
- Now open the circle using your wand (or your athame).

You can leave the card on your altar or in a visible place (e.g., on your nightstand), for a whole Moon cycle. If you aren't able to so, put the card or rune back with the rest, and let the Universe work its magic for you, now that you have sent your intention.

Day 15: Banishing spells

Banishing spells are meant to remove harmful or unwanted things from our life. These can be as simple or as complex as you want them to. We all have things we would like to see disappear from our lives, and a little magical help is always welcome.

For today's spell you will need the following:

- A candle, ideally black, but a white one will do.
- A piece of paper.
- A black ink marker or pen.
- Matches or a lighter.
- A cauldron or a fire safe container where you can burn a piece of paper.

First of all, come up with something you would like to

remove from your life. Please reflect about it and write it down *exactly* the way it should happen. Be careful with your wording.

For example, if your neighbor has an extremely loud dog, step back before writing something like *"I want my neighbor's dog to disappear"*. You probably don't want anything bad happening to the dog. You just want him to *stop barking* so loudly in the middle of the night, while you are trying to sleep. So, in this case, it would be better to write *"I want my neighbor's dog to stop barking loudly at night"*. In spells, wording is key.

For this example, I will create a banishing spell for something silly, like the ants which seem to invade my kitchen over and over again, no matter what I do. I will print a picture of the ants, or write *kitchen ants* on a piece of paper. You can use the same spell pattern to banish anything you want, just by substituting the text in brackets.

- Set your altar.
- Cast a magic circle with an athame, wand or the tips of your fingers.
- Light the candle in the middle of your altar. Place the paper which states *what* you want to banish next to the candle, in a cauldron or other fire safe container.
- Read your spell three times:

I banish you now, [unwanted ants who invade my kitchen].
Go away and never come back.
Disappear from my sight, disappear from my life.
Go away and never come back!

- Now burn the paper with the candle until it becomes unreadable.
- If you have no way to do this safely, just tear the paper in tiny pieces.
- Close the circle.
- Go outside and bury the ashes (or tiny pieces

of paper) as far from your house as you can.

If you have nowhere to bury them, the second best option if to flush them down the toilet or throw them in a trash can as far away as you can (wait for them to cool off to avoid an accidental fire and make sure this won't clog your toilet!).

If you can't do this right away, you can keep them in a covered glass jar and do it later. Just beware that the spell won't start working until you get rid of the ashes.

Third Weekend: Meditation Quick Start Guide

Third weekend practice: meditation

Meditation is a great way to calm down your mind, cope with stress and connect with your inner self. Daily meditation will help you connect with your dormant psychic powers because it silences the hundreds of mundane thoughts which overpopulate our mind as we go about our daily lives. We keep thinking about our shopping list, what we are going to make for lunch, what errands we have to run, who aggravated us and why, why we are so sorry for ourselves, and the list could go on and on endlessly. Mundane thoughts, and especially negative thoughts, tend to happen in a loop, repeating themselves to no end. It is actually exhausting!

Studies have proven that meditation is great for our mental and physical health[9] [10]. It might not be a practice exclusive to Witches, but it is one of the most helpful practices you can add to your daily routine: it is inexpensive and the results can be very rewarding. Meditation is useful before using any divination method (e.g., before performing a Tarot reading), and before spellwork. It helps you focus and

---

[9] *Wiley Online Library,* **Meditative therapies for reducing anxiety: a systematic review and meta-analysis of randomized controlled trials** *(online), seen on: https://onlinelibrary.wiley.com/doi/abs/10.1002/da.21964 (2017).*

[10] *Science Direct,* **Three-year follow-up and clinical implications of a mindfulness meditation-based stress reduction intervention in the treatment of anxiety disorders** *(online), seen on: https://www.sciencedirect.com/science/article/pii/016383439500025M (2017).*

connect with your intuitive inner self.

How to start meditating:

In order to meditate you don't really need any*thing*, apart from (at least) five minutes of undisturbed peace. You should strive for fifteen to thirty minutes per day eventually.

It is easier to start with guided meditations, but you don't need them if you don't want to. During a guided meditation you just listen to a voice in a recording, which usually guides you through a scene you visualize in your mind. Many meditations start by helping you relax each part of your body and go on to imagining yourself immersed in a very soothing setting, such as a walk along the shore of a beach or a forest. You can follow them effortlessly, and they are much easier for a beginner than just keeping your mind empty for a while.

Some people don't like guided meditations and prefer to meditate on their own (more on this below).

Where to get guided meditations:

Search for guided meditations on the internet: many can be find on pages such as YouTube. There are also free and paid meditation and mindfulness apps you can download to your smartphone or tablet. Find one you feel related to: there are meditations for any issue you can think of: most of them are meant to help you relax, but you can find meditations to release anger or sadness, to meet your angelic guides, to visualize yourself during past lives, to clear past issues, etc.

If you later discover that you enjoy the practice of meditation, you might consider joining a meditation or mindfulness group in your community. This kind of groups are also a great way to meet like-minded people near you.

The simplest way to meditate:

If you don't enjoy guided meditations or you can't find any that you like, you can still meditate on your own, in silence.

Sit down on the floor with your legs crossed. You can have soft background music or just listen to your environment quietly.

Fix your eyes on a point in front of you and try to still your mind. A great way to do this is to light a candle and look at its flame. Looking at the fire in a mantelpiece is a good idea, too, or observing the running water of a creek or the leaves of a tree dancing in the wind.

Thoughts will probably start to flood your mind. You don't need to make an effort to stop them: just *watch* them. Whenever a new thought appears, you just label it silently: *"thought",* and let it pass. Don't let the thoughts unfold, just watch them like a movie unrelated to yourself, and wait for them to pass.

This kind of meditation can be harder at the beginning, but it is very effective, and it has the advantage that you can practice it anywhere without any tools at all (not even headphones).

When to meditate:

I like to meditate right before I go to bed, because my home can get quite busy during the day, and it's hard to find the necessary peace and silence until everybody else goes to sleep and phones stop ringing.

If you are a morning person (I envy you), you can set your alarm fifteen minutes earlier every morning and use this extra time to squeeze a short meditation into your morning routine before you have breakfast. It will help you start your day calm and energized, and you will have more patience to face the challenges of the new day. Some people end up substituting their first morning coffee with meditation, so it might be worth a try.

Setting your meditation goals:

Put meditation on your calendar or set an alarm every day at the same hour. Start by meditating five minutes every day. It is better to do it every day for a shorter time than to meditate only once a week for one hour. If you manage to find time for five minutes a day, try to add one more five-minute session in the morning, evening or after lunch. Or try to expand your five-minute meditation to a ten-minute one. Try to keep this a part of your daily routine from now on.

Apart from meditating, I encourage you to find time for a cleansing and manifesting bath (or shower) as described in the previous chapters.

CHAPTER 4:
The World Around You

Witches are much more than spellcasters: they are listeners, carers and guardians of nature and all its living creatures. Their job on this planet is to observe, protect, help others and make good use of the goodness provided by our generous environment. Witches look at the stars, the Moon and the planets; numbers, animals, plants and all kinds of events and seeming coincidences. Nothing happens just by chance in a Witch's eyes, and they are able to discover hidden messages where ordinary people see nothing. It is exciting when you are able to read signs and help yourself with the clues the Universe sends you.

Day 16: The Moon And The Goddess

Some scientists would tell you that the Moon is *just* the satellite of the Earth. But then, many modern Witches —and there are scientists among them, too—, see the Moon as much more than that. Some see the Moon as an image of a/The Goddess, with its waxing, full and waning phases representing the three shapes of the Great Mother, the feminine side of the energy which composes our whole universe:

The waxing Moon has the growing energy of a maiden, as impersonated by maiden goddesses such as Artemis/Diana, Persephone, Rhiannon…

The full Moon, with its blooming force, can be compared to a fertile mother, just like the Goddesses Demeter or Gaia. All women in their fertile years are considered to be Mothers in this sense, whether they have children or not. This is the moment in a woman's life when her energy is at its peak: her career and family lives are flourishing, and her physical strength is usually at its climax, just like the light of the full Moon.

The waning Moon seems to be shrinking: the strength of its light is declining and the Moon seems to be nearing its disappearance, although in truth it is just going into a more introspective phase. This Moon has become old and wise, and it knows the end is near; but it also knows from experience that this is just a phase. The New Moon (also known as black Moon) is not really an ending, just the last step before the beginning of a new cycle. This is the Crone stage of the Goddess. In case you were wondering, Witches don't give any negative connotations to the word *Crone*: being a Crone is actually an honor, because it means a woman has gone through all the phases of life, and is now old and wise: she is past her child-rearing years, and can devote herself fully to her craft and her psychic development. All post-menopausal Witch women are considered Crones. The most well-known Crone Goddess is Hecate, (Hecate goes through the three phases of maiden, mother and crone, but is often represented as a Crone). Hecate is often named the Goddess of the Witches.

Women are cyclical creatures, much more so than men (although many men report changes with the Full Moon, too). Our bodies are deeply affected by the Moon: many women menstruate with the Full Moon and ovulate with the New Moon. In maternity hospitals it is said that there are more births on Full Moon nights. Many people report how they (or their babies) sleep better or worse depending on the current phase of the Moon. The Moon affects our bodies, just like it affects the tides: we are made mostly of water, just like the sea, so it shouldn't come as a surprise that the phases of the Moon can affect our moods and the behavior of certain bodily functions.

Why are Witches so fascinated by the Moon?

When Witches revere the Moon, they are mostly honoring it as a reflection of the Great Goddess, who is a representation of Divine Feminine energy. They also consider it a mighty and unending source of power, which affects all living creatures on our planet.

Phases of the Moon.

Since the dawn of humanity, the Moon has fascinated us, humans, with its shining light and its changing phases. The Moon seems to shine, but the light we see is not the Moon's own light: it is reflected from the Sun. Its shape also seems to change, but this is just an illusion: only its position changes, and with it the amount of light reflected from the Sun. All of this gives the Moon a magical aura of mystery and sometimes, a warning about possible deceit, which is a constant in human nature too. The mysterious Moon energy is the opposite of the open, masculine, extroverted energy of the Sun, and this is also reflected in the Moon card in a Tarot deck. The Moon card reminds us that, sometimes, things seem different in the veiled light of the Moon, and it warns us not to fall prey of fear when darkness surrounds us, because everything in life comes in cycles, and the darkest hour always precedes the light of a new day.

These are just a few of the reasons why Witches are fascinated by the Moon. Its protective light saved many practicing Witches from death during the Burning Times, so this is one more reason to be thankful to the Moon.

Today's assignment:

Today I would like you to find out the current phase of the Moon. Find a calendar or do an internet search to discover when the next full Moon is expected. There are some apps you can install on your phone or tablet, which will notify you whenever the Moon is about to enter a new phase. There is one which will actually *howl* like a wolf right before the full Moon!

Ideally, get a paper calendar (or print one out) and mark on it all the New and Full Moons of the current year.

With your journal, reflect on the past Full Moons and see if you can remember any changes on or around those dates.

- Do you sleep better/worse on full Moon nights?
- Is your period synchronized with the Full Moon?
- Do you feel tired right before the Full Moon?
- Are there any other patterns you can notice, comparing your calendar/personal diary with a Moon calendar?

If you can't find any connections, don't worry. Track the next Moon cycle from beginning to end and note on your journal any feelings you might note in yourself, your pets or your children.

Note: many modern women living in urban environments can't notice any synchronicity with the Moon. This can be due to the excessive artificial lightning in our environments. In order to maximize your connection with the Moon, try to keep artificial light to a minimum in your home after sunset, and sleep in a dark room with drawn curtains and lowered blinds. On Full Moon nights, let the light of the Moon enter your bedroom, so that your body can get used to the natural night lighting differences. If you use your phone or computer after sunset, get one of those blue light filter apps which darken the screen depending on the Sun cycle.

Day 17: The Magic of The Moon

There are many ways you can work with the Moon to enrich your magic. Maybe you will not be able to try the techniques described in this chapter today, depending on the current phase of the Moon at the moment you are reading this, but you can still mark on your calendar the spells you would like to try, and on which dates.

The strongest Moon energy can be found during the nights of full Moon. Some Witches call them Esbats and consider them a holiday to be celebrated. I don't use the terms Esbat or Sabbat myself: I prefer to call them, plainly, full Moon nights, but this is just a matter of personal preference.

Making Moon Water

When we make Moon Water, our purpose is to **infuse water with the energy of the Moon**. In order to do this, <u>leave a glass jar or bottle under the light of the full Moon.</u> Allow it to bathe in the moonlight for a minimum of one hour, or for the whole night if you prefer. Some people like to add a crystal to their water (just check it is safe to do so, because some crystals —like tiger's eye, to name one— can leave toxic residues in your water, while others may dissolve in your water and plainly disappear). I simply set one or two clear glass bottles under the light of the Moon and pick them up the next morning. If I want to prepare crystal-infused Moon Water, I tape the crystal of my choice to the bottle (from the outside) with ordinary *cellotape*. You can also buy special, double-chambered bottles for this purpose, but my system seems to work just as well for a fraction of the price. Depending on where you live, the quality of the water and the temperature inside your house, you might have to keep your Moon water refrigerated if you don't drink it immediately the next morning.

You can drink your Moon water to infuse yourself with Moon energy in the morning (I really love to do that), put it on your skin, add it to your bath water or use it in spells.

Using the Moon's energy for spells

Always note the current phase of the Moon before you start a new spell, because it might enhance or diminish its effectivity.

- **Waxing Moon Spells:** during the days and nights when the Moon is growing, choose spells of growth and abundance. This is the best time for money spells (growing your fortune), etc.

- **Full Moon:** at this point the Moon's energy is the strongest and spells performed on a night of full Moon (or the night right before the full Moon), are supposed to be the most effective.

- **Waning Moon:** when the Moon is decreasing, it is better to choose banishing spells. This is the time for healing spells (banishing illness), and other spells which are meant to remove any harmful things from your life.

- **Black Moon:** when the Moon is absent, some Witches refrain from using magic at all. This is a time of introspection and meditation. Some even say spells can go awry if performed during this period. I wouldn't go so far as to say that, but their potency might be affected. I would rather wait at least for the first slice of Waxing Moon, unless a spell is really urgent.

Cleaning Your Tools

1. Why clear the energy of your magic tools?

All talismans, jewelry and tools used for spellwork tend to absorb energy from their environment. When you buy a ring, a Tarot deck or a wand, whether used or new, they might carry some residual energy from the people who crafted them, transported them or even touched them until they came to you. This energy can be especially strong when you buy or inherit second hand jewelry or home decorations, which were worn or touched by a certain person for a very long time, or at a time when that person was going through very strong negative feelings. If you suspect there might be any undesirable energy attached to the object, it is always a good idea to cleanse it before using it for magic or putting in on yourself or inside your home.

The same happens when you carry a certain object with yourself daily, or when you use your crystals and tools often. They might get "tired" after performing intensive energy work for a while and absorb your moods or those of people around you. That's why it's generally advisable to recharge your tools and crystals, and clear the energy they might have absorbed after some time of use.

One of the easiest ways to do this is to set your crystals, divination tools, etc., under the full Moon. You can simply set them on your window sill (the inner side will be fine, if you are worried they might fall or be stolen), or on a small table in your yard. Set them out at sunset and pick them up at sunrise. Don't worry if you can't pick them up exactly at sunrise: if you want to sleep in and leave them a while longer, that should not undo the energy clearing (some people will disagree, but there is no universal *right* and *wrong* in Witchcraft, so do what suits you best). Just beware that some crystals are sensitive to rain and will need to be kept under a roof or a glass dome, while others, such as amethyst, can become discolored when set under the direct light of the Sun for long periods of time. Glass spheres should never be left under direct sunlight because they could start a fire.

The idea that leaving your items outside after sunrise could be counterproductive may be a remnant from the Burning Times, when Witches had to be careful not to be seen doing anything suspicious by their neighbors. Speaking of which, your neighbors may raise a brow or two if they happen to see your extensive collection of magical tools while driving past your house!

If you want, you can say a brief spell when leaving your items under the full Moon, such as:

> *"Oh silver Mother Moon,*
> *take these offerings in your sacred womb,*
> *make them pure, all negativity be now removed,*
> *under your magic white light, oh mighty Moon."*

If you happen to acquire something new and you simply

can't wait for the full Moon to start using it, there are other ways to cleanse the energy of an object. A very simple option is to keep a small container with Moon water in your refrigerator. If you need to cleanse an object, fill a cup with Full Moon water, put the object inside and say the Moon clearing spell (see above). Leave the object inside the cup, under the light of the Moon, for a whole night. Rinse it in the morning.

Day 18: The Power of the Sun

The power of the Sun: the solstices and equinoxes

Witches revere nature, which is ruled by the Earth's yearly turns around the Sun. Most things in nature happen in cycles, and a good way to observe the periodic nature of the seasons is to pay attention to solstices and equinoxes. The seasons of the year are of foremost importance for human life on this planet, although, nowadays, many of us, especially city-dwellers, may have forgotten about the necessity to live seasonally. The prevalence of electricity and artificial lighting, greenhouse produced vegetables and air conditioning/heating have made most of us oblivious to the passing of the seasons. Some affirm that we, humans, have become stronger than nature and the seasons are of no importance to us anymore: but anyone who has survived a natural catastrophe will be able to tell you how fast nature can wipe out human dwellings and leave us hungry and cold, our little electrical appliances turned into useless plastic bricks. We can't outsmart nature in the long run. Witches are aware of it, and so they revere, respect and celebrate the seasonal changes.

Solstice and equinox festivals have been celebrated since Neolithic times. Many of them were adopted by other faiths, with different and sometimes very similar names.

There are two solstices each year:

The winter solstice, or the longest night (that is, the day with less daylight hours, when the Sun reaches its lowest point at midday), which happens around the 21st of December. The winter solstice was celebrated long before other concurrently occurring holidays such as Christmas, the Roman Saturnalia and many other holidays were later accommodated on the same or similar dates. Witches celebrate the longest night of the year with candles and lights, which make darkness shorter and brighter and help call back the spring. It is customary to prepare warm, rich food, specially baked goods typical of the colder months.

The summer solstice, *Midsummer's Eve* or the longest day of the year takes place around the 21st of June and celebrates the power of the Sun when it is at its maximum, and the goodness and plenty brought to us by the warmer weather. In many traditional cultures it is celebrated by lighting a fire and bathing in the sea at midnight, under the light of the moon. In European Catholic faith, this tradition is still practiced as Saint John's Eve. Other traditions celebrate with summer flowers and fruits, moonlit fires and songs.

Solstices mark the beginning of the winter and summer, respectively. Pagans celebrate the solstices and in Anglo-Saxon or Germanic traditions usually name them **Yule** or Yuletide (winter solstice) and **Litha** (summer solstice). I actually enjoy the simplicity of calling them solstices and don't really use the terms Yule and Litha unless talking to other Pagans.

There are two equinoxes each year:

The spring equinox, on the 21st of March, also known as **Ostara** in Wiccan circles or Easter for Christians. On the spring equinox we traditionally celebrate the fertility of nature and all its plants and creatures. Some well-known symbols of fertility are eggs (a seed of life which will soon burst, turned into a living creature) and bunnies (the hare, related to Goddess Eostre or Ostara).

The fall equinox (called **Mabon** by many Pagans), on the 21st of September, when we celebrate the harvest of the fruits of the Earth after a long, warm summer, and we start to store and preserve food for the coming colder months. We make jams, pies and juices, and enjoy the fruits of late summer.

Samhain

Samhain, or the Celtic New Year's Day, coincides with All Hallows' Eve and the newer Halloween on the last day of October, and is <u>considered by some Witches the most important Pagan celebration of the year</u>. This is **the moment when the darkness reaches its peak**, and when the veil which divides the world of the spirits and the dead (also known as the Otherworld) and that of the living becomes thinner. Intuition is heightened and the souls of those who passed are said to be reachable on this night. This is a celebration of endings and a day to honor and remember or loved ones who already crossed over. Samhain marks the end of plentiful warm days, as crops and warmth become just a memory from the past and the cold, bare winter takes their place.

All of this makes for a great evening to practice magic, especially for releasing what we don't want any more in our life or reconnecting with the departed.

The other three mid-season festivals:

These holidays are not recognized by all traditional Witches, although most Witches of Christian, Celtic or Anglo-Saxon background will probably be acquainted with them, specially the first day of May.

- ▪ **The 1st of May, or May Day**, is an important day in many cultures, and it marks the very middle and highest peak of the spring. It could be considered the opposite side of Samhain. It is also known as ***Beltane*** in Celtic culture. This is a beloved wedding date for Pagans, when many handfastings (Pagan weddings) are celebrated to honor the wedding of the Mother Goddess and the Father God, symbolizing the pairing of all creatures of nature during springtime. Dancing around Beltane fires and flower covered poles (maypoles) are popular ways to celebrate the first day of May.

- **Imbolc,** or Brigid's Day, around the 2nd of February, marks the middle of Winter, and overlaps with Christian Candlemas and Roman Lupercalia, and it is usually a purification celebration meant to end the winter and attract fertility and health. Traditionally, candles are lit, symbolically bringing back the light of the Sun.

- **Lammas**, on the 31st of July, is a harvest holiday which marks the middle of the summer. After harvesting the grain, delicious food is baked and eaten to celebrate the generosity of nature and the fruits of hard work.

Today's task:

Try to find out about this year's exact date for each of the solstices and equinoxes and note it down in your journal.

Try to remember any familiar or folk traditions which were or are still practiced around those dates by your family, your ancestors or the people who live in your area. For example, you may want to research the origins of Christmas trees and Christmas lights, or research about your local village farmers' festival, which happens every year in the middle of September. In some places they put up May Crosses, made of wood and covered in flowers, which vaguely resemble Pagan maypoles. Make a list of customs you already had and feel free to add your own personal touch: pay attention to your personal traditions, from baking cookies to lighting candles on special days, and add any new traditions you would love to add to your yearly celebrations. You may have been celebrating Pagan holidays unknowingly!

Day 19: Planets and Stars: the World of Astrology

Celestial bodies tend to be a fascinating subject for most Witches. Many books have been written about Astrology, a discipline which attempts to describe how celestial bodies, their movements and the position on a given time, can influence human destiny. In order to become a good astrologer, you will need many years of study. Still, having at least a basic knowledge of astrology will be helpful for you as a Witch, and so the goal of today's chapter is to provide you with some wide Astrology concepts you can use as a stepping stone.

You will soon notice that **there isn't just one unique Astrology system in the world**. Western, Vedic and Chinese Astrology are probably the best known. **The information you will find in this chapter is related to Western Astrology**. If you find any of the other systems more suited to your cultural background and personal beliefs, don't hesitate to use today's session to research about them instead.

Astrology is a form of divination which tells us things about people (or events) based on their date of birth, which is used to build a natal chart, or a schematic drawing of the sky which describes the positions of planets and celestial bodies at a certain moment (usually, at the exact hour a person was born). Astrological charts can then be interpreted, and a good astrologer might be able to tell you many interesting things about yourself, your past, your present and maybe even your future inclinations, just by looking at your natal chart.

Elements of an astrological chart:

In order to understand and astrological chart you will need to have at least notions of the different signs, houses and planets. When they all combine in a chart, we can start to extract meaning from them. The study and interpretation of those combinations is what makes astrology a lifelong study for many of us.

1) The 12 zodiacal signs

Most Westerners are already acquainted with the twelve signs of the Zodiac and will be able to name their Sun sign and maybe even the traits related to it (although many of them won't know that it actually is their *Sun* sign!). This is the sign in which the Sun can be found at the moment of your birth, and it changes during the year, as the Earth orbits around the Sun. Many of us have already heard, for example, how Taurus people are stubborn or Leo can be bossy; although this is just a generalization and you might actually meet a very docile Taurus and an obedient Leo, depending on the positioning of the rest of planets on their chart.

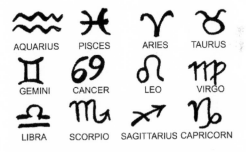

1. **Aquarius**, *January 21 to February 19*. Friendly, original, intellectual problem solvers, unpredictable.
2. **Pisces**, *February 20 to March 20*. Calm and intuitive, very sensitive and compassionate. Sometimes too weak-willed.
3. **Aries**, *from March 21st to April 20th*. Strong characters, energetic, achievers, adventurous and confident. Can be too impulsive.
4. **Taurus**, *from April 21st to May 20th*. Patient and stubborn, artistic, loving and reliable. Can be jealous and resentful.
5. **Gemini**, *May 21 to June 21*. Imaginative, talkative, lively and adaptable. Can be nervous and inconsistent.
6. **Cancer**, *June 22 to July 22*. Emotional and loving, imaginative, protective and trustworthy. Can be too

moody.

7. **Leo,** *July 23 to August 22.* Ambitious, strong, generous and warm-blooded, faithful and passionate. Can be too patronizing.

8. **Virgo,** *August 23 to September 22.* Reserved and hardworking, shy, meticulous and analytical. Sometimes worries too much, can be too much of a perfectionist.

9. **Libra,** *September 23 to October 22.* Easy going and sociable, charming, sometimes too changeable, indecisive.

10. **Scorpio,** *October 23 to November 22.* Analytical and intuitive, passionate, although secretive and sometimes resentful.

11. **Sagittarius,** *November 23 to December 21.* Smart and very sociable. Can be excessively optimistic or irresponsible.

12. **Capricorn,** *December 22 to January 20.* Traditional and practical, very disciplined and careful. Can be too pessimistic.

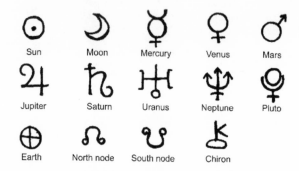

2) The planets and celestial bodies:

1. **The Sun,** rules the sign of Leo and it is related to the fire of life, strength, and the self.

2. **The Moon,** rules the sign of Cancer, emotions, feminity, intuition.

3. **Mercury,** signs of Gemini and Virgo, rules

communication and intellect.

4. **Venus**, signs of Taurus and Libra, is related to love, beauty and material goods and pleasures,

5. **Mars,** ruler of Aries and, partly, Scorpio, is related to power, action and sometimes aggressivity.

6. **Jupiter,** ruler of Sagittarius and, partially, Pisces, related to abundance, knowledge, optimism and expansion.

7. **Saturn**, ruler of Capricorn and, partially, Aquarius, related to discipline, rules and limitations, and pessimism.

8. **Uranus**, ruler of Aquarius, related to inventors, scientists and individualists,

9. **Neptune**, ruler of Pisces, related to spirituality, imagination, dreams, and in the worst case addiction and delusion,

10. **Pluto,** ruler of Scorpio, related to transformation, healing, life and death, and obsession.

11. **The North Node**: in a chart, it means what potential you have.

12. **The South Node**: it is related to your karmic past.

13. **Chiron** is a comet which is also known as *the Point of Healing* when reading charts. Chiron symbolizes the parts of your life which need to be healed so that you can become a stronger or better person.

3) The 12 houses

The twelve houses are 2-hour (or 30 degrees) divisions in an astrological chart, which is drawn as a circle (360°/24 hours). Each individual house has a certain meaning, and we check which planets we can find in each of them in order to find out more about a person and their potential.

1. **1st house:** your self-identity and your approach to life, all the "firsts" in your life. What you **are.**

2. **2nd house:** value systems, self-worth, money and material goods. What you **possess.**

3. **3rd house:** communication, the mind, siblings, social sphere. What goes on in your head.

4. **4th house:** home, mother, family and security. What makes you feel safe.

5. **5th house:** love, joy, creativity and children. What you create.

6. **6th house:** health, work and service given to others. What you do daily (for others).

7. **7th house:** marriage, contracts, business partners. The people you link yourself to.

8. **8th house:** healing and inheritance, sex and intimacy. What you share or have in common with others.

9. **9th house:** travel and teachers, cross-cultural influences, religion. Where you expand yourself towards.

10. **10th house:** public image, career, achievements, the father. What you achieve (material).

11. **11th house:** friends and hopes for the future. What you contribute to the community.

12. **12th house:** your inner self, spirituality, secrets, your past and karmic debts. Your spiritual goals and dreams.

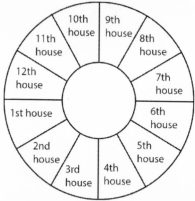

Today's assignment: working with your Astrology natal chart

Find out your exact date and hour of birth and try one of the many Astrology chart calculators available online. Just find a free generator and type in the day and the exact hour you were born in order to get your natal chart. If you can, print it out and add it to your journal.

How to start working with your astrological chart:

Your chart is composed by a circle, divided in twelve sections which represent the twelve houses (see previous illustration).

- You will notice the symbols of the planets and celestial bodies distributed among the houses. This is the position they could be found at exactly when you were born.

- Take a pencil and try to write the name of each one next to it.

- Afterwards, pay attention to where each celestial body is located. What house is your Sun in? Where is your Moon? What about the planets?

- Look at the descriptions of the celestial bodies and try to connect them to the house they are in. For example:
  - You notice Venus in the 4th house.
  - You check the list and see that Venus is related to love and material pleasures.
  - The 4th house is related to home, family and security.
  - Possible interpretation: *someone with Venus in their 4th house will probably enjoy staying at home. This person can have a stable, loving relationship with their family and strive for a calm, homey life.*

Analyzing your own chart is the best way to start learning Astrology on your own. Afterwards, if you find the subject interesting, you can get yourself an Astrology book or course to deepen your knowledge.

Day 20: Numerology

Today we are going to work with numbers and their meanings. If you hated Math during school, please don't run away just yet: this is going to be easier, I promise! We will briefly tackle Western Numerology, also known as Pythagorean Numerology because of its inventor, the Greek philosopher Pythagoras.

Numerology, just like Astrology, can reveal many interesting things about yourself and the people you know, providing you make the effort to decode whatever the numbers are trying to tell you. They can let you know about difficulties to watch out for, what your personality is like, your hidden potential, etc.

Just like astrologers draw charts, numerologists look at numbers present in names, dates of birth or even addresses, in order to find out more about people and situations. The main numbers studied by numerologists are called **core numbers.**

Today we will calculate the **core numbers** for Mary Ann Smith, born on September 19th, 1986[11]. Afterwards you can do the same with your own name and date of birth.

CORE NUMBERS:

Life Path number, this is a number which broadly describes the good (and sometimes not-so-good) events which might take place during your life. Let's calculate Mary Ann's Life Path number:

09/19/1986 (MM/DD/YYYY): we first reduce the day, month and year to a single number.

$09 + (1+9) + (1+9+8+6) = 9 + 1 + 6 = 16 = 1+6 = 7$.

Name or Expression number, this number explains how your name affects your destiny.

---

[11] *A fictional character.*

Write down the full name and substitute each letter by the numbers from the table below:

M A R Y A N N S M I T H = 4 + 1 + 9 + 7 + 1 + 5 + 5 + 1 + 4 + 9 + 2 + 8 = 56 = 5 + 6 = 11.

Personality number: this number describes what you look like from the outside: that is, the first impression others get when they first see you.

In order to calculate it, add all the consonants in your name (M + R + N + N + S + M + T + H).

The Soul or Heart's desire number: this is a number which gives us information about your inner self and your deepest dreams and feelings: this is the part of yourself which very few people know.

Add up only the vowels in your name (A + Y + A + I).

Birthday Number: this is a number which defines what you allow others to see when they look at you: it tells us about your exterior appearance and how you present yourself to others. It is just the day you were born, and it will be a number from 1 to 31. In Mary Ann's example, her Birthday Number is 19.

MEANINGS OF LIFE PATH NUMBERS:

This is a list which includes very broad meanings for the main numbers you will encounter when working with the core numbers. You can use it to interpret, for example, the life path number of a few of your friends and relatives, and see if the descriptions match.

- **1** are leaders, innovators, inventors, ambitious and charismatic people.
- **2** are peacemakers. They are mediators,

listeners and good judges.

- **3** are creative and communicative, friendly and social.
- **4** are good planners, practical people, trustworthy and hardworking.
- **5** are adventurous free souls who love changes.
- **6** are nurturers, idealistic, always there to help others.
- **7** are smart and analytical investigators and thinkers.
- **8** are ambitious and capable, very hard working.
- **9** are generous and compassionate, helpers, humanitarians, non-materialistic.
- **11** are similar to number 2, but amplified. More intuitive, etc.
- **22** are similar to number 4, but amplified. They are intuitive and great builders.

Today's task:

- Calculate your own core numbers like in the example.
- Calculate your life path number and the ones of a few people you already know, and look at their description in the list.
- If you want, you can try to find more information about Numerology and how to choose proper dates for important events, which numbers are most compatible, etc.

Fourth Weekend: Animal Companions

Pets and familiars:

Let's just talk about pets and familiars today. If you hang out with other Witches relatively often (even if it's just on social media, it counts!), you might have heard about their *"familiars"*. But what does that exactly mean? Is that just another word for *"pet"*?

Well, the short answer is **no**, it is absolutely not the same! Sometimes a pet can be or become a familiar, but most pets are not.

The word *familiar* comes from the expression "familiar spirit". These are supposed to be helpful spirits who take animal forms in order to assist and protect a Witch. They can present themselves as dogs, cat, crows or, actually, any animal you can imagine. The difference between a pet and a familiar is the depth of the connection and communication said Witch shares with the animal. It is said that familiars have no *owners,* just **human companions.** *Familiars* can help Witches with their spells, warn them from danger, show them important information and help them in the most unexpected ways.

Animal companions assignment:

1) Do you have a pet? Describe it in your journal. Do you think your current pet is a familiar spirit? If it's not, you can try to deepen your current connection. You can do this by observing it more closely, snuggling together more often, sharing time and going to places together, trying to communicate (verbally or not), etc.

2) Are there any wild animals where you live? Try to find pigeons, ants, ladybirds, bees or squirrels. There are more animals than it might seem, even in the middle of the biggest city. I actually knew an old lady who had a very special connection with a hedgehog who came to visit her every evening in her garden.

3) This weekend, go for a walk and pay attention to all the animals you see. Listen to them. Try to hear what they are trying to communicate. Are they angry? Excited? Hungry? Look at the paths drawn by the ants in the park. Observe the dance of the ducks in a pond, the shape of a passing flock of birds. Is there a stray cat who looks at you from the other side of the road every morning? Maybe you should greet her and bring her some food? Write in your journal about the living beings you met during

your walk, and specially about how you felt about them, whether they might have been trying to give you any signs concerning the current state of your life, etc.

It has been a long week, hasn't it? I think we deserve a rest and some time to celebrate all these achievements.

The rest of tasks for this weekend:

- Put your journal in order during the weekend and re-read the passages you found more interesting (or confusing).

- Try to work with the Moon, especially if you are lucky enough to have a full Moon during this weekend.

- Plan ahead for the next year, using your journal. How could you celebrate the coming solstices and equinoxes?

- Don't forget your weekly cleansing bath or shower.

- Make sure you have some coarse salt in your kitchen for next week's exercise.

- Do the previous activity about familiars.

CHAPTER 5:
Spellwork 101

Spellwork, as in casting more or less complex spells, is probably the best known Witchcraft practice, and the one which attracts the most novices to the craft. Still, many people live a Pagan life and do very little or no spellwork at all. They prefer to cultivate a deep connection with nature, the Moon or their deities, or practice the arts of divination and cleansing instead. Contrary to the general beliefs, there is no requirement to cast spells in order to be a Witch.

True Witchcraft spells can be very different from those depicted in novels and movies. You probably know already not to expect sparks, whirlwinds or flying balls of fire. True spells are comparable to deep meditation and manifestation practices. They usually work in a silent, inner way under the surface. Sometimes they are incredibly fast and effective, despite the lack of Hollywood flashiness. **Ingredients and processes are important, but true magic originates in the Witch herself. The magic *is* the Witch, and the only indispensable ingredient is her will.** Some Witches become so advanced in their practice that they develop the ability to cast spells with their mind only: they can forego candles, herbs and altars, and just use the power of their mind instead. Some Witches, on the other hand, enjoy the process of creating intricate rituals and casting complicated spells for their whole life, notwithstanding their years of experience.

Written spells, with carefully selected words, ingredients, and steps to follow, can be easier to perform for a beginner, because ritual helps us to focus and appeal to the powers which lie dormant within ourselves. Each step of a ritual helps the Witch focus her intentions and can make the whole process more powerful. Even if you have to work harder to find certain ingredients and follow a given protocol, this will assist you tune our mind into the frequency of magic, positivity and manifesting. This is why **I strongly recommend you to follow each step of a spell while you consider yourself a beginner,** and start introducing your personal changes after you get a little practice.

Day 21: Cleansing

Learning to cleanse and consecrate yourself and your tools

We already discussed cleansing with the Moon in Chapter 4. As we already saw, *cleansing*, when used as a magic term, refers to removing all residual energies and entities which may have remained attached to an object before it landed in your hands. If you are wearing a ring, who mined the metal? Who shaped the ring? Who gave it to you? Do you think all those people were thinking happy thoughts while doing their part? Probably not, so there is a good chance that a certain amount of bad energy attached to the ring until it came to you, or while you were using it.

When working with magical tools, we really don't want anybody's residual energy influencing the outcome of a spell. That's why it's so important to cleanse them properly before doing anything else. There are many ways to cleanse your things, although some are faster and more practical than others. They can all be effective, but it's good to try a few when you are starting out and see which one makes you feel better.

If you have been following the exercises from this book, you will have had a few **cleansing baths** yourself by this time. This is not coincidental, and it serves a purpose: to cleanse your physical and ethereal body from old energies and attachments which don't serve you anymore and can become a heavy burden after a while. The goal is to start your new life as a Witch as a new, better version of yourself. Some of the gentler methods described below can be used to cleanse yourself, such as bathing under the full Moon or rubbing your body with sea salt. The rest are meant to cleanse objects or spaces, as we will see.

ENERGY CLEANSING METHODS:

Cleansing with the Moon

You can find out more about cleansing your tools under the full Moon by referring back to <u>Week 4</u>.

Sage and incense

Sage sticks are a very popular cleansing method, in large measure because of their ease of use. Cleansing a space or an item with smoke is also known as **smudging** (a practice which dates back to Indigenous peoples). You can buy sticks made of dry sage leaves tied with a thin string made of natural materials. Usually, white sage is used for this purpose, but any sort of the same plant will do. There is controversy over whether white sage is endangered or not: at the time of this writing we weren't able to find a well-grounded answer to this question. Anyhow, try to find ethically grown and sourced sage sticks (rather than wild harvested varieties), or, even better, <u>grow and dry your sage yourself</u>: it is a very easy to grow crop, even on your balcony. Please beware, not everybody enjoys the smell of sage smoke, while others, such as allergic or asthmatic individuals, can't tolerate it at all, specially indoors. In case of doubt, buy only a small amount the first time and see whether you like it or not. Sage is sold in holistic shops (if you are lucky enough to have one in your area) or otherwise online. Sometimes you can find potted sage in supermarkets and grocery shops.

In order to use a sage stick you must set it ablaze carefully and blow out the fire after a few seconds, so that you have a smoking stick with no flame. Keep a fireproof bowl handy, so that you can catch the embers and put down your stick if you must, and have a plan in case you had to put it out quickly (maybe keep a bowl of water near, for emergencies). Once your smoldering sage stick starts to smoke gently, you can surround the object you want to cleanse with smoke spirals. Some Witches start the ritual by smoking themselves first.

Sage sticks are great for cleansing spaces, such as houses and buildings in general. Just remember to leave a window open for the stale energy to get out, and to check for smoke detectors first.

Sage smudging stick.

If you can't get any sage, you can try smudging with **incense sticks**, which should be available in most supermarkets. Try to get hold of natural —if possible organic— incense. Dollar shop incense sticks are usually filled with artificial colors and perfumes and don't contain any real herbs or essential oils.

Never use smudging in hotel rooms and overall in any building equipped with smoke detectors —let alone planes or vehicles—, because it can set off the fire alarm or even the sprinkler system, and cause you lots of trouble. In these cases you can use sound, light, prayer or any of the methods discussed below.

White light

This is one of my favorite cleansing techniques, because it can be done virtually anywhere, it's fast, free and very discreet, and you need no tools at all.

- Take the object in your hands or concentrate your vision on it, blurring out the background.
- Take a few deep breaths.
- The next time you inhale, imagine a flow of powerful white, cleansing column of energy coming down from the sky and entering your body at the crown of your head, then exiting through your extended hands.

- Direct this white light towards the object you want to cleanse.
- Imagine the object surrounded in white light, like a thick bubble around it.
- Imagine this white light dissolving all the residual energies on this object. Keep the bubble for as long as you deem necessary.
- Once you sense the object is clear, you can keep the white light for a bit longer, so that the object can absorb its clear energy.
- Afterwards just release the bubble back into space.

Running water

If you live near a stream of water or the sea, you can just put your tools in the water for as long as you feel necessary for them to be cleaned.

I like to clean them first with tap water and soap. Actually, I clean everything under tap water before using any of the methods described here. For me it's like a pre-cleansing to remove actual dirt and easier to remove energetic gunk.

Put the item under the stream and visualize the running water as a white jet of energy which sweeps away the energy which doesn't serve you anymore.

Note: if you intend to use this technique, just make sure your tools won't be damaged by the water. Some crystals, such as selenite, are water soluble and washing can damage them.

Salt

Salt has been used to ward off evil for centuries. I prefer to use sea salt because it contains the force of two elements: earth and water (the salt itself belongs to earth, but it came from the ocean, which is water). Other Witches, though, favor rock salt because it's extracted from the depths of the Earth. Use the one you find more convenient.

There are many ways to use salt in Witchcraft, such as:

- Putting a container with salt on top of your desk in

a busy office, so that it can absorb negative energy,

- Rubbing your damp skin with salt in the shower, to remove bad energy which might have got stuck to your body (it makes a great peeling, too).
- Burying a small object (such as a ring or a small stone) in a bowl of salt, like you would bury it in the earth (see below).
- Making a circle of salt to keep yourself protected while inside (more about this in the next chapters).

Burying in the earth

This is actually one of my *least* favorite methods of cleansing, because it takes a long time. But it is really good for crystals and objects which you have tried to cleanse before and still seem a little off. By burying an object directly in the soil, you will allow it to release its stale energy into it and absorb the grounding and calming energy of mighty Mother Earth. Some practitioners like to bury their tools for a whole Moon cycle, while some seem to see results after one week already. Use this method for crystals which can't be put under running water or under the Sun. Ideally the object should be in direct contact with the soil, but you can also wrap it before burying it. Don't forget to mark the spot so that you can find your things afterwards.

The Sun

This method will work well for you if you live in a very sunny place and you have the possibility of leaving your things outside for some hours, in full sunlight. Just be careful when using the power of the Sun to cleanse your tools, especially if you are working with crystals. Crystal balls are well known for provoking fires when exposed to sunlight (they concentrate the rays of the Sun, so be very careful to keep yours covered with a piece of cloth, even indoors), and some crystals, such as amethysts, can be discolored when put under the Sun for long periods.

Your task for today:

Gather your Witch tools and try to cleanse at least one

or two of them. Try at least two of the methods described in this chapter. Afterwards, write down what you experienced and describe the whole process, step by step, in your journal. Hold the cleansed object in your hands and close your eyes. Answer the following questions:

- How did the object feel *before* the cleanse?
- How did it feel *after* the cleanse? Was there any difference?

Day 22: Grounding and Shielding

GROUNDING

Are you *grounded*? What is *grounding*, anyway?

Sometimes our energy seems to be scattered all over the place. We are nervous, our thoughts bounce around our head, and we seem to be unable to accomplish anything[12]. This is the opposite of feeling grounded. When you deal with your daily problems, and especially if you are empathic and you easily pick up energy from other people, you quickly become ungrounded.

On the other hand, **when you are grounded you feel calm, centered and focused. You can see clearly and decisions become easier to take. A grounded person feels peaceful and emotionally stable.**

Ideally you should ground yourself every morning when you wake up, and every night before you go to sleep. This will help to keep your energetic body clean and strong. If nothing else, it is imperative to ground and cleanse yourself before and after doing any kind of energy work for others, and before and after practicing divination and spellwork.

There are many ways to ground your energy, but the easiest to use are:

Grounding Meditation

Do this meditation while standing or sitting cross-legged

---

[12] *Of course, this might be caused by stress and many other things, so in case of doubt, check with your doctor first.*

on the floor.

- Close your eyes and imagine a cord made of white or golden light which runs from the top of your head to your sit bone, where your root chakra is located.
- Imagine how this cord extends down until it reaches the Earth and goes inside it. If you are in an apartment, imagine how your cord of light goes through all the concrete floors, the basement and the foundations, until it reaches the earth under the building you are in.
- Imagine the cord getting roots and becoming firmly anchored in the warm, welcoming and protecting Earth.
- Keep breathing and see how your energy becomes connected to the one of the planet, as it turns steadier, calmer and stronger. You are safe, at home. During this step it is very important to breathe deeply and slowly.
- When ready, open your eyes, make yourself comfortable and try to feel the difference.

Walking barefoot

Another way of grounding yourself is walking barefoot on the grass or the Earth. If you can, close your eyes and imagine yourself becoming connected to the Earth, just like described in the former meditation.

Grounding with crystals

Some crystals, such as smoky quartz and other black-colored crystals, can help you stay grounded if you wear them on yourself or keep it near you often.

If you have no such crystals, you can try to find a big rock in the forest or next to the sea and bring it indoors. You can touch it with your bare hands when you need to ground, and sense how the residual energy leaves your body through the hands, while you connect to the Earth through the rock. Remember to put your rock out under each full Moon in order to keep it cleansed, or leave it under the Sun from time to time. Dark rocks are better for this purpose.

Note: when buying dark crystals, and specially smoky quartz, get them from a reputable vendor. Distrust cheaper pieces, which are often irradiated in order to give them a dark brown color artificially.

SHIELDING

Shielding is a magical way to protect yourself from harmful energies. Shielding is not the same as cleansing: while shielding prevents negativity to reach you, cleansing removes it once it has become attached.

In order to become shielded you must first ground yourself as described in the previous passage.

Once you feel properly grounded try to imagine a shield of white light surrounding you and protecting you from all evil. If interacting with other people tends to drain you, create a white light shield every morning after you wake up.

Some people use crystals to shield themselves. Some of the best known are amethyst, tourmaline, black onyx and labradorite, although there are many more. Still, I find crystals alone are not enough. I think white light shields are more effective, or better, the combination of both methods. If you wear crystals, remember to cleanse them regularly, because they will eventually become saturated and stop working.

Today's task:

Today, —or even better, tomorrow morning before you leave the house—, ground your energy and create a white light shield around yourself.

See if it makes a difference while you go about your daily business.

At the end of the day, write about it in your journal. Did your magical shield work well? Did you notice it becoming weaker in the company of certain people, or at certain places?

Day 23: Magical Symbols

The longer you practice Witchcraft, the more symbols you are bound to encounter on your path. You can use them on yourself, in your spells, for protection and even as a way of finding like-minded brothers and sisters in the most unexpected places. From time to time, unknown Witches smile at me when they notice my triquetra pendant.

Most of the symbols we will see today have ancient origins and have been used for diverse purposes over the course of history, so you may find different meanings depending on the source you check.

The Pentacle

Probably, the best known symbol of Witchcraft —and one of the most misunderstood by those unconnected to it— is **the pentacle**, also known as **pentagram**.

A pentacle is a (usually upwards), **five-pointed star**, enclosed in a circle. The five points symbolize the four Elements plus Spirit, and can also be read as a reference to human nature (the star resembles a person with their arms open). When the five-pointed star becomes enclosed by the circle, it additionally symbolizes the relationship between human and Universe.

Pentacles are a sign of Pagan faith. They are definitely not "satanic", nor evil, nor do they attract demons to the wearer (don't ask me where I got this one). A pentacle is actually meant to bring good luck. Sadly, people in some communities still fear a simple pentacle, due to ignorance and misinformation. If the people around you are very close-minded or extremely religious, it might be unsafe to wear a pentacle in public, as it could attract trouble-makers (but no demons, though). Some Witches living in such communities rather sew a pentacle to their underwear, wear it in a long chain hidden under their shirt or have small tattoos made in discreet and hard-to-see spots. Another option is to opt for less obvious symbols, like the ones we will see below.

The Triple Moon

The Triple Moon symbol is related to the three phases of the Moon (waxing, full and waning) and sometimes can refer to Goddess Hecate in her three forms (Maiden, Mother and Crone), also known as the Triple Goddess and the patron of Witches.

Celtic knots are very popular among Witches, especially those of Celtic heritage. The one you will see most often is the triqueta (above, left), which is also related to the Triple Goddess, and the triskelion or triskele (above, right), for similar reasons.

The Tree of Life

This symbol has become so popular in the last years that I doubt anyone would name you a Witch for wearing one. It does have many meanings. It can represent the connection of all things in the Universe (how we are all one, and so each of us can be considered divine, or a piece of God). It also depicts one of the main principles of magic, which is *"as above, so below"*, meaning that (Wo)man and God are one, what happens in Heaven happens on Earth, and human will can be manifested in the material plane, because that, which happens within you, can be materialized outside, too.

Stars

Apart from the five-pointed star in a pentacle, six-pointed stars (hexagram, Seal of Salomon or Star of David) are used in magic as a talisman. Seven pointed stars (heptagram) are often a symbol of **faerie magic** (they are also called a *fairy* or *elven* star).

The seven-pointed star can also be a symbol of the magic order of Thelema, or the seven planets known to ancient alchemists.

Norse Symbols:

These are symbols related to the Norse culture and mythology, often used by Asatru Pagans. The Mjölnir, or Thor's Hammer (left picture), is a symbol of protection. The Valknut (right picture) symbolizes God Odin and the transition between life and death.

Egyptian Symbols:

Egyptians were known for their deep knowledge of magic, and many Egyptian gods and goddesses are still revered by modern Witches nowadays. The symbol above these lines is the Eye of Horus, which is used for healing spells, among others.

Today's task:

Have a look at the symbols presented in this lesson.

- Have you seen any of these symbols anywhere before? Maybe you even own a t-shirt or a pendant featuring one or more of them? You may even find the logo of a company near you surprisingly resembles one of the symbols depicted in this chapter.

Make a new chapter in your journal and try to draw a few symbols, writing their name and meaning next to them. Decorate them and color them: use it as a coloring meditation. Coloring is a great way to relax and calm down the flow of thoughts in our heads.

Day 24: Casting A Circle

A ritual circle is an enclosed energy space where you can practice magic. The space isn't confined by walls or fences, but by invisible boundaries set by the Witch who cast it. Magical circles are used to enclose the energy, for focus, and to offer protection to the magic practitioner.

There are many ways to cast a circle and they all can work. Some Witches enjoy long rituals while others just need one minute to cast a circle with their mind. I will show you two ways of casting a circle. Both are valid, and both can be effective; but I recommend you to use the longest one at the beginning. Once you get the hang of it, you can simplify or expand the process as much as you want.

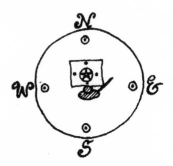

Casting a circle the quick way:

Find a relatively open and empty space in your home or in nature. Take a few deep breaths and concentrate in the spell you are about to do. Raise your hand, pointing your index finger or your wand, and draw a circle clockwise, imagining you create a sphere of white light around yourself while you do it.

When you finish your magic work, don't forget to release the circle. Just repeat the process, this time counter-clockwise.

Casting a circle the proper way:

- Find an open space in your home or in nature.
- Look at the Sun or use a compass to locate the North: place yourself so that you are facing North.
- Set a small altar on an altar cloth, with the representation of each of the Elements facing the right direction (Air–North, Earth–East, Fire–South, Water–West).
- First, you will "Call the Quarters" or the protective forces of the elements. In order to do this, lift your wand and turn in the correct direction, as mentioned in the invocation:

> "I call upon the Spirits of the Four Elements,
> I call the Element of Air (face East),
> the Element of Fire (turn South),
> the Element of Water (turn West)
> and the Element of Earth.
> (Turn north and end the circle where you started it, overlapping it slightly)."

> "I thank the four Elements for assisting me in my magic practice today. Thank you, thank you, thank you."

(This is known as "Calling the Quarters").

- Now, if you wish to, you can ask your Goddess, or God, or both, to help you and remain with you while you practice your magic. Don't forget to thank them three times.

■ Afterwards, start casting the circle. You will draw a circle with your wand, **slowly and clockwise**. Once you are done, say:

■ *"This magic circle is cast, here and now.*
So it is, so it is, so it is.".

■ Your circle is now cast, and you can start with your spell, or whatever energy work you wanted to do.

■ Don't leave the circle while you work (see below why).

CLOSING THE MAGIC CIRCLE

■ Once you finish, you will have to close the circle. You will do the same, just in the opposite order.

■ First, thank the Gods for having been there with you.

■ Then, thank the Elements:
"I thank you, four Elements,
for having been here with me.
Thank you, Element of Water! (Face West).
Thank you, Element of Fire! (Turn South).
Thank you, Element of Air! (Turn East).
Thank you, Element of Earth! (Face East)."

■ Finally, draw a **counter-clockwise circle** with your wand, starting from the North. Once you have finished, just say:

"The circle is open now. So it is, so it is, so it is."

Salt circles:

Some people use coarse salt in order to draw a physical circle on the floor, and mark the four directions with four candles inside the circle. I have done this only once, and the circle created was extremely strong. I could feel the energy vibrating in that room even after it was closed. But let me tell you, sweeping and mopping all that salt afterwards was beyond exhausting!

A *word of caution:*

You are not supposed to leave a magic circle without opening it first. That could break the circle and cause your spell to fail. Some Witches are afraid that a broken magic circle can become a portal for unwanted energies to enter our plane.

If an emergency occurs, depending on how urgent it is, you can do two things:

1. **Try to close the circle** as described in the "quick" magic circle technique.
2. **Run if you must and *go back in time*** when you can. After the emergency is over, when you finally find a moment of peace, sit down in meditation, with your eyes closed. In your mind's eye, imagine you go back to your magic circle. Imagine the moment when you were interrupted. Then, visualize yourself closing the circle properly. If you can, thank the Elements and the Gods aloud, and wave your wand as you close the circle.

If you still perceive the circle wasn't properly closed, you can go back to the place you started at (if possible. If not, do it somewhere else, but state aloud your intention of closing the still-open circle, before you start). Set your altar again and cast a new circle, but using salt instead of your wand. Just hold a bowl of coarse salt in one hand and throw a line of salt on the floor, drawing a white circle around yourself. Then close the circle with your wand and sweep the salt once you have finished the whole process. Salt is very protective and salt circles are very strong. You can also sage the whole space for extra safety.

Day 25: Using Correspondences

Tables of correspondences are extremely helpful when creating a new spell or making changes to an existing one. Simply put, they are tables where you can check which are the ideal components to manifest your intention. They list colors, numbers, planets, herbs, etc., which are related to a certain intent. Witches usually make their own tables of correspondences, and document them in their book of shadows or journal. We have already discussed a little of Numerology, Astrology, candle magic, etc., so you have some material to start creating your own tables.

Today's task:

Copy the table below in your journal and fill it in with the information from the previous pages. Don't worry if you don't know all the answers: you will find the solutions in <u>Chapter 8</u>. Still, I encourage you to leaf through this book. It will help you remember the correspondences much better than just looking at a table composed by someone else.

TYPE OF SPELL	COLORS	HERBS	CRYSTALS
Romantic love			
Passionate love			
Health			
Money			

Fifth Weekend: The Principles of Manifestation

Manifestation is not very different from spell casting: it is just done slightly differently. Simply put, **manifestation is using the power inside of ourselves to create our own reality.** The key concepts are:

- Visualize your goal as clearly as you can.

- Translate your goals into a sentence which describes them (an *affirmation*). For example: *"I have a wonderful relationship with my mother".* *"My dog is perfectly healthy".*

- Always see the positive side of things. Don't allow pessimistic scenarios to flood your mind. **Avoid affirmations which include pessimistic words**, and double negations, which can be confusing. Examples of affirmations to avoid: *"My mother and I don't* argue *anymore".* *"My dog has no* fleas *anymore".* These contain the words *argue* and *fleas,* which automatically force you to visualize arguments and flea-infested dogs. Your goal is to fill your mind with harmonious mother-daughter moments and happy, healthy dogs, not the opposite.

- Try to repeat your affirmation as often as you can. You can set yourself reminders or objects around your house which remind you of your goal (for example, pictures which represent what you would like to achieve). There are affirmations apps you can install on your phone.

- Always say thank you for achieving your goal even before your wish has come true. *"I am thankful for the wonderful relationship I have with my mother".*

Manifestation techniques are great when used along with magic spells. I usually combine both and write my spells with manifestation principles in mind, that is, I try to use positive sentences and avoid negative words in them.

Always say *thank you* at the end and visualize the outcome clearly before it happens.

This Weekend's Task

This weekend take some *me-time* with your journal. What would you like to manifest in your life?

- Think about your life and make a list of things you would like to achieve. What are your goals for:
    - Your finances,
    - Your career,
    - Your health,
    - Your partnerships,
    - Your personal growth.

Now open your journal and write those things like they already happened. This is a key concept in manifestation: we must *believe* the miracle has already happened and give thanks before it actually materializes. This way, our mind sets in motion the necessary processes for the things we want to start happening. **Gratitude** is a very strong positive force to aid in manifestation. So, you will write in your journal:

Some of my journals.

Thank you, Universe, for... (add here the things you would like to see happening. Substitute the word *Universe* for the one you feel most related to).

CHAPTER 6:
Spellwork II

If you have been reading one book entry per day, this chapter will mark our last week together. We will dedicate the last few days to learning some practical and versatile spells. You will be able to customize them to suit your needs, or write your own spells if these don't resonate with you.

Before casting a spell, copy the text into your journal, and modify it as needed. Make sure you have all the ingredients nearby before you start.

A *few notes on writing your own spells:*
1) Vocabulary: some Witches feel the need to use archaic English in their spells. I don't, because in my view, a good-working spell should come from the heart and reflect the caster's personality. But if you *do* think your everyday thoughts in Shakespearean English, for all means, please write your spells that way, too! But if you don't, and you almost giggle when trying to pronounce words such as *thou, thee* and *thy*, don't feel obliged to speak like Prince Hamlet while practicing your magic: there's no need.

2) Rhymes: you might have heard that a good spell should rhyme. I agree with this. Musicality and repetition give extra strength to a spell. But sometimes, when you are writing your own spells, you simply can't make it rhyme properly. Don't worry: if it doesn't work, it doesn't. You can still use it. The world will keep turning: even for us, lousy poets.

3) Writing it down beforehand: always take a moment to write down a spell before performing it. I know it is very tempting to just start talking and describing your wish as you go, but, trust me, it's not a good idea. I have tried it and failed. Why? Because spells must be specific and made with intent. If you just start talking to your altar about your wishes like it's your best friend, the Universe may get confused (I don't really blame it. My thoughts can be quite random sometimes). Just write everything down in advance and make sure there are no possible misunderstandings, to avoid an unexpected outcome in case your wish were to be fulfilled word by word.

Day 26: Sigil Magic

Sigil magic uses symbols called **sigils**, which are specifically drawn to contain the power of our intention in each of their strokes. You can search for pre-made sigils in books or the internet, but I don't really recommend you to do so: the most powerful sigils will be those created by yourself, because they will be imbued with your intent.

There are many ways to create a sigil, and most of them will work. We start by stating the sigil's intention. For example:

"Laura will invite me to her party."

Try to use the principles of manifestation, like we saw in the last chapter, that is: stating your wish like it has already happened/it is already happening, and avoiding negative words. Additionally, try to avoid statements such as *"I want to"* or *"I wish to"*. Be clear and concise.

Once you have a short sentence which describes the intention you wish to manifest, you have to start to transform it into a sigil, that is, a drawn magical symbol.

How to transform written words into sigils

1) Draw each word

The first method consists in separating each of the words and creating a doodle for each of them. Try to create abstract drawings to represent them. For example, you can draw a stylized balloon to represent the word *party* or a few sticks to represent *Laura* from the example above.

Afterwards, just try to superpose the doodles and create a shape out of them. Add them to each other in random ways, some to the left, some inside each other, some on top, etc.

Redraw the resulting shape a few times, simplifying it a bit more each time, until you get a symbol which doesn't resemble the original doodles anymore. This will be your sigil.

2) Meditate on your sentence

Find some time to meditate in peace. Write your wish in the top half of a sheet of paper and hold it in your hands. Let the words flow from your hands to your brain until you start to perceive colors and shapes in your mind's eye. Imagine the words travelling through your heart before they reach your third eye chakra. After doing this exercise for a while, you will be ready to start drawing. Take a pencil and start doodling automatically. Don't think: just doodle. You can look at the paper, but don't make any efforts to draw anything concrete. Draw absent-mindedly, like you do when you are talking to someone on the phone. Just try to keep your wish in mind while you do it. Smooth and connect the shapes, erasing what you esteem shouldn't be there. Embellish it as much as you want. And remember: it's your sigil and you are not going to show it to anyone, so don't worry if the result is not a work of art.

3) Start with the letters in your sentence

Pick a few random letters from your sentence. For example, you can pick every fourth letter (or second, or fifth. You can use Numerology to decide which one). In our example, this would be:

"*Laura will invite me to her party.*"

A I E H R

Try to create a shape by putting those letters together. Some can be in cursive, some bold, some highly ornate, etc. If one letter reminds you of a certain shape (e.g., your "O" turns out like a spiral) just go with what your intuition tells you and correct it so that it resembles the shape you are thinking about.

Examples of sigils.

How to use a sigil:

Once you have your sigil, record it in your journal, next to its meaning. After that, you can start using it.

1) Keep it near you so that you can see it often. Whenever you see it, repeat your wish in your mind. For example:
    1. Draw your sigil in the last page of a notebook,
    2. Use it as a mobile phone background picture,
    3. Put it in a photo frame and put it on your nightstand, etc.
2) Put it on your altar while you do a spell related to it. Once you finish the spell, burn it or tear it in tiny pieces and bury it. Some Witches flush them down the toilet if none of the previous options is available.

Your task for today:

After all this time together, I'm sure you can guess what today's task is! You will have to create your very own sigil and once finished draw it in your journal. Have fun!

Day 27: Freezing Spells and Cord Cutting

Most Witches are loving and understanding people. They strive to be patient and helpful, and do their best to heal their relationships whenever possible. Still, not everybody around us is kind and understanding, and there are times when toxic relationships must be left behind if we want to keep our personal growth (and our sanity). The two spells below are used in such cases, especially after all "ordinary" ways have been exhausted (that is, after you have tried to tell that person nicely to leave you alone, etc.).

Important note: *if someone is trying to cause you damage your first line of action should be to find real (tangible) help: contact your friends, teachers, boss, authorities, or whoever could defend you fast and efficiently. Spells are just something you do along the rest of common-sense practical measures, and you should never depend on them to keep you safe. None of the spells listed in this book are proper ways of dealing with life-endangering situations and persons.*

FREEZING SPELLS

A *freezing* or *freezer spell* is used when you want to keep someone away from you. It may be an annoying relative who criticizes you or invites themselves to your home without calling first, an irritating classmate or co-worker, or anything along those lines.

You will need a small container with a lid (a small mason jar will do) and a picture of the person, with their name written on the back. If you don't have any pictures, you can also write their name on a paper.

- Fill the container until 2/3 with water.
- Then immerse the picture in the water while you say the following words (substitute *John Smith* with their real name):

> *"John Smith,*
> *In here your name is trapped,*
> *Remain blocked in this ice,*
> *Your venom will now freeze,*
> *Your damage, paralyzed.*
> *You are gone,*
> *And I'm at ease."*

- Put on the lid and leave it in a deep and forgotten shelve of your freezer. It should start working soon after the water solidifies.
- After a while, if you judge the relationship has

cooled off enough, you can thaw it and bury the contents. If the irritating person comes back, you will have to repeat the process.

CORD CUTTING SPELLS

When we interact with others, a part of their energy can get attached to our ethereal body. Some describe this attachments as **invisible cords which join people together due to shared experiences**. These cords are intangible and can extend from one continent to another. Depending on how deeply your shared experiences touched you both, the more resistant these cords will be.

Sometimes cords are useful: for example, when a mother and her child are joined by an energetic cord which helps them remain aware of each other even when they are apart. However, energetic cords can become a burden if they keep bringing back painful memories from people we would rather forget. In such cases, it can be a good idea to attempt a cord cutting spell. Think it over before you do it, because the results could be irreversible. Still, new cords can be created on a daily basis, but once the old ones are cut, they won't reappear on their own. Some cords are tough to cut, though! You will see by yourself.

Cord Cutting: What you need:

This is one of those spells which work well even when performed only in your mind. But for the first times, it's better to use a piece of black thread to represent the cord we are going to cut, and a sharp knife or scissors to do it.

- Prepare your space and altar as usual to perform a spell.
- Imagine the person you need to cut cords with

standing in front of you.

- Take the black thread and put it between them and you.
- Imagine how this cord extends from the top of your head to the top of the other person's head. It is a thick, black cord, which connects your thoughts and feelings.
- Now take the scissors (or boline) in your dominant hand, while you hold the thread with the other hand, and say:

> *"I cut the bond between us,*
> *nothing joins us anymore,*
> *farewell, never come back.*
> *We are apart, in peace you go."*

- Slowly, cut the cord in two.
- See how, after the cord is cut, the other person's silhouette starts to fade until it disappears or flies away like a leaf in the wind.
- Afterwards, you must dispose of the remains of the cord. If you want, you can burn it and spread the ashes far away from your house. If you can't burn them, then just bury them in the earth, as far away from you as you can.

Day 28: Money Spells

Money spells are very popular, but it's wise to tread carefully when using them. You should be very prudent when asking the Universe for money, because there are ways of coming across money which can be painful, sad or damaging. Imagine for example you wished to receive $10.000, but you didn't add any extra information to your wish. You might end up having an accident, for which you would receive—you guessed it— a $10.000 (or similar) insurance compensation. Or you might lose a family member and receive $10.000 in inheritance. For this reason, please consider the wording of your spell carefully, and always add at the end *"may this money come without harm to anyone"*.

MONEY SPELL

You will need:

- Ten small coins (one cent each will do).
- A candle (green, gold or white)
- An envelope.

When to perform: during the waxing Moon, to increase money.

Where to perform: outside, in a garden or forest, next to a big tree if you can.

Before you start:

- Wash the coins well with water and soap and then cleanse their energy. You want to receive *clean* money, which will come to you from honest sources and will not cause you remorse or guilt. While you wash them, repeat in your head: *"clean money, honest money, I wash you now"*.
- Write on the envelope the exact sum of money you need. If you need a new car, research which one you would like to get and write its exact price on the envelope. Try to be realistic. Don't try to manifest a Ferrari if it's completely out of your league.
- Then say:

Money comes easily and quickly to me,
And the fortune I need is now here,

- Start putting the coins one by one in the envelope as you say:

  One tenth of my fortune,
  Two tenths of my fortune,
  Three tenths of my fortune,
  Four tenths of my fortune,
  Five tenths of my fortune,
  Six tenths of my fortune,
  Seven tenths of my fortune,
  Eight tenths of my fortune,
  Nine tenths of my fortune,
  Ten tenths, and that's all I need.

  My money grows now,
  As I plant it here.
  Grows under the Moon,
  Will come soon to me.
  With no harm to anyone,
  I bury money seeds,
  And may this clean money
  Become mine so quick!

  So it is, so it is, so it is.

- As you read the last paragraph bury the envelope somewhere where it will be left alone for at least one whole Moon cycle.
- Water it as often as you can, if possible daily, or at least weekly.

Day 29: Spells to Assist with Healing

Before we start, as these are delicate matters, I need to write an important disclaimer: *if you are unwell, please consult a doctor and follow their advice. This book doesn't contain medical advice. The information given here is not meant to substitute the care of a physician, nor to replace any medication. Consider this information as provided for entertainment purposes only, and, if you decide to use it, understand that you do so under your own responsibility solely, and no-one else but you can be held responsible for the outcome.* If you feel sick or unwell, just call a doctor. This is why we have them!

This said, people have used energy to try to speed up or aid healing since the dawn of humanity, be it in the form of prayers, laying of hands or anything else. Sending wishes of healing is an age-old custom and just like you can buy greeting cards with the text *"get better soon"*, we will use our magic to send our very personal and "virtual" *get well soon* magical *card*. It's just the way we'll send it will be slightly different.

You can find studies[13] which show small health improvements in patients who were prayed for from a distance (most of them along their allopathic treatment) in comparison to those who were not.

Ask for permission if you pretend to perform a healing spell for someone else. Some people who belong to other religions might not appreciate it, or could even become angry in case they found out about your spell. To be safe, don't perform spells for third persons who didn't ask for your help first.

When to perform a healing spell: perform the spell during a waning Moon in order to banish what you don't want.

Candle color: green or white.

---

[13] *PubMed, A randomized, blinded study of the impact of intercessory prayer on spiritual well-being in patients with cancer, (Online). Seen on: https://www.ncbi.nlm.nih.gov/pubmed/22894887 (2018)*

PubMed, A randomized double-blind study of the effect of distant healing in a population with advanced AIDS. Report of a small scale study, (Online). Seen on: https://www.ncbi.nlm.nih.gov/pmc/articles/PMC1305403/

Number of items: 3

What you need:

- 3 green candles (if you don't have any, use white candles).
- An engraving tool (a boline, a needle, etc.).

How to proceed:

- Ideally, wait until the Moon starts to wane and do this spell under the light of the waning Moon.

- Set your altar as usual, marking the four cardinal directions.

- When you feel ready, cast a circle as described in the previous chapters.

- Recall the problem you want to banish. Then take your candles and needle and carve on the candles:

  - On the first one, carve the name of the person who needs healing (your name, if it is you),
  - On the second candle, carve the part of the body to be healed. If you are not sure, you can write "full body and mind", although the more specific, the better,
  - On the third candle, write the words *"perfect health"*.

- Recite the following spell:

> *Brigid, Apollo and Sekhmet[14],*
> *I call on you, to seek your help.*
> *On (Name)'s behalf,*
> *Be here tonight.*

(Wait for a few seconds and pay your respects to the Gods and Goddesses).

> *(Name)'s health is now restored,*
> *And illness from her body dislodged.*
> *(Name), recover your strength!*

(Take the matches and start lighting the candles as you recite).

> *As I light this first candle,*
> *(Name)'s body is free of pain.*

(Light it and visualize suffering leaving the person's body).

> *As I light this second candle,*
> *(Name)'s (part of the body)*
> *Shines in perfect health.*

(Light the candle and visualize the person completely healthy and happy).

> *And with this third candle,*
> *I complete this spell.*

(Light the third candle and say thanks to the Gods and

---

[14] *Depending on your religious views, you can substitute as necessary. Ex. I call on our Lord Ganesha, etc. If you find Sekhmet's energy too strong, you can invoke just Brig.*

Goddesses for their healing help).

> *Perfect health is here.*
> *Perfect health will stay.*
> *So it is,*
> *So it is,*
> *So it is.*

Let the candles burn out. If you can't stay in the room for so long, blow them out and resume the spell later as seen on Chapter 3, to avoid leaving your candles unattended.

Day 30: Love Spells

As we saw in Chapter 1, I am mostly against ordinary love spells where a person is unknowingly tied to someone else. In my opinion, they violate one of the partner's free will and are doomed to fail and backfire. As the saying goes, *"be careful what you wish for".*

I'd rather recommend *"lighthouse" spells* instead. With this kind of spells, you try to make yourself more visible to any potential partners, but you don't pick someone in advance. This is fair enough because they are still free to fall in love with you or not. You just help more people to notice you among the crowd.

The Lighthouse Spell to Find Love

You will need:
- A red or pink candle,
- A bowl of water with rose petals (an even number).

When to perform it: during the waxing Moon.

Procedure:
- Set the candle safely into the bowl and read the spell three times before lighting it:

I call you now, my dear one,
come to me from wherever you are.

My heart is open like a rose,
to give and receive true love;
affection, care and romance,
may they come to me at once.

- Light the candle and hold your hands over the flame from a safe distance.
- Feel the warmth of the candle on the palms of your hands and imagine it as it travels from your palms, along your arms, until the center of your chest.
- Imagine a warm and bright pink light in the middle of your heart, shining, becoming bigger, and surrounding you in pink light and love.
- Afterwards, you can choose to leave the candle burning or blow it out. But **keep the pink light burning in your heart**, to help your future partner find you.

This spell will keep getting stronger as the Moon waxes and be at full potency during the full Moon.

Sixth Weekend: Creating a Magic Pouch

Magic pouches are also known as *"mojo bags"* or *"gris-gris bags"* in different traditions. They are little pouches you carry with you at all times in order to achieve a certain goal.

In order to make a magic pouch you will need a small, pre-made bag, or a piece of cloth and a string (the cloth can be square or circular). Ideally, choose a bag color which matches your intention (a green bag for money, a red one for love, etc.). Don't make it too big, because you are going to carry it constantly, hidden, on your person.

You can buy mojo bags which have already been filled by someone else, but it is much better to make one yourself for your specific situation. Just decide what you want to achieve and find a small object which represents it. If you want to find a new home, you could put a small key inside, or a small piece of brick. Check correspondence tables and decide which herbs or stones could work well. You don't need to put many objects inside, but they all must have a meaning and a purpose. Choose an odd number of items (3 or 5 works well).

Examples of things you can use:

- Cinnamon or coins for money,
- Dried rose petals for love,
- Rosemary and nettle for protection.

Once your bag is filled, close it tightly with a string and put it around your neck or hide it in your clothes (use an inner pocket, the strap of your bra, or any other hidden and handy place). You should carry your pouch so that nobody can see it, and show it to no-one. If it is discovered by others, it may stop working. Magic pouches are usually treated almost like a living being and therefore should be *fed* from time to time. This means you will have to add small herbs and trinkets every other day. Leave some empty space in your mojo bag to allow enough place for the items you will be feeding it throughout the days.

Once the magic pouch has served its purpose, you can bury it. Don't just throw it away in the trash because that would be disrespectful.

CHAPTER 7:
Wrapping It All Up (In Silk)

If you came this far, I would like to congratulate you. Our small tour of the world of Witchcraft has come to an end. But this doesn't have to be the end: just like Death in the Tarot is not just an ending, consider this your new beginning. Now you have a book of shadows to work with, and many ideas to put into practice. I hope you enjoyed working through this *Solitary Witch's Green Book,* and I wish you all the best while you walk the ancient path of the wise women and men. Embrace your magic and use it sensibly. Practice makes perfect. Don't worry if you don't get everything right in the beginning: just keep trying, and you will become a master eventually. Keep writing about your rituals, findings and observations in your journal, and follow the phases of the Moon and the cycles of nature. Become one with them.

From Witch to Witch, from human to fellow human, I want to thank you for your interest in magic and for the time you spent reading this book.

May the divine light of knowledge and fairness shine on you at all times.

CHAPTER 8:
Useful Lists And Tables

Runes Keywords

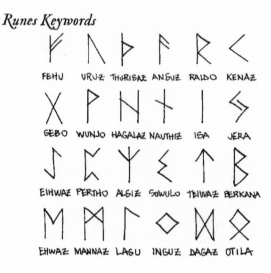

1. Fehu: literally "cattle". Meaning: wealth, money and assets, material gain, fertility.
2. Uruz: lit. "strength". An ox, physical strength, health, stability.
3. Thurisaz: lit. "giant". Related to God Thor. Defense, harm, conflicts, protection.
4. Ansuz: "wisdom". Related to Odin. Learning, wisdom, divine guidance.
5. Raido: "wheel". Journey, traveling, movement, messages, a good time to start.
6. Kenaz: "torch". Guidance, truth, revelation, shining a light on something.
7. Gebo: "gift". Love, positive partnerships,

agreement, contract, exchange, charity.

8. Wunjo: "wind". Joy, blessings, good news.

9. Hagalaz: "hail", harsh weather. Risks, things collapsing or not going the expected way, accidents.

10. Nauthiz: "need". Obstacles, delays, losses, endurance, hard work.

11. Isa: "ice". Things coming to a halt, cooling, loss of energy, blockage, waiting for the ice to melt.

12. Jera: "year". Harvest, payment or reward after an effort, peace.

13. Eihwaz: "yew-tree". Rebirth. Restart. Death. Only the strong will survive (like the yew tree survives the winter).

14. Pertho: "dice". Destiny, mystery, secrets, taking risks.

15. Algiz: "elk". Protection against evil, good luck.

16. Sowulo: "sun". Victory. Achievement, positive outcome.

17. Teiwaz: "arrow". Courage, fighting, achieving justice, battle, victory.

18. Berkana: "birch". Purity, birth, growth, woman, mother.

19. Ehwaz: "horse". Progress, journey, moving forward.

20. Mannaz: "human". A man or mankind. Altruism. Relying on yourself.

21. Lagu: "lake". Feminine side, water, intuition, dreams.

22. Inguz: "the god Freyr (also known as Ingwaz)". A man, husband, protection, (positive) conclusion, old situations resolve.

23. Dagaz: "day". Growth, revelation, clarity, opportunity.

24. Otila: "home". Heirloom, house, property, ancestors, comfort.

Tarot Keywords

MAJOR ARCANA[15]

0. THE FOOL: symbolizes a new beginning, starting something new with the innocence of a child.
1. THE MAGICIAN: you have the power to create something new with the tools you already have around you or within yourself.
2. THE HIGH PRIESTESS: this is the moment to pay attention to your intuition: you probably know the answer to your question already. Just listen quietly to what your heart has to say.
3. THE EMPRESS: indicates a mother; fertility, feminity and abundance. Nurturing something or someone. Being creative.
4. THE EMPEROR: he usually represents a father figure or a person of power; masculinity, authority, taking control of a situation.
5. THE HIEROPHANT: instructs you to learn from or take the advice of recognized institutions. Finding an experienced mentor to help you on your quest.
6. THE LOVERS: a sign of a lucky union or partnership.
7. THE CHARIOT: victory, control, a fast ride (usually towards triumph).
8. STRENGTH: this card tells you that the necessary strength to solve this matter is already in you. You can do it: be strong.
9. THE HERMIT: recommends you to find time to be alone and search for the right answer within yourself. Find the light in the darkness.
10. THE WHEEL OF FORTUNE: a sudden change in direction, usually a lucky and sudden change if things were not going well. Also, the end of a cycle.

---

[15] *If you use playing cards, you will not have the Major Arcana cards.*

11. JUSTICE: the truth will be finally known, each one will get what they deserve, law will prevail. Refers to contracts and legal matters.

12. THE HANGED MAN: expect delays, wait and be patient. Try to look at this matter from a different point of view.

13. DEATH: the end of something, which brings a new beginning. A transformation, metamorphosis. Very rarely means actual death.

14. TEMPERANCE: finding balance and/or health, acting with moderation, being patient.

15. THE DEVIL: being a slave of materialism or vices and addictions. Obsession and excessive focus on material possessions and carnal desires.

16. THE TOWER: a sudden and mostly unwanted but unavoidable change. Something happens which shakes the foundations of your world. But it had to happen.

17. THE STAR: (new) hope, the calm after the storm, a moment of peace.

18. THE MOON: falling prey of your fears, letting yourself be fooled by illusions. Someone is hiding things from you. Don't give credence to everything you see because things are not always what they seem to be. Sometimes things seem scarier in the light of the Moon, that is, when you are in the middle of a dark situation, but they will look different if you shine a bright light on them.

19. THE SUN: success, positivity, children and childhood, childlike happiness.

20. JUDGEMENT: a time of rebirth; becoming a better version of yourself, being forgiven for your sins.

21. THE WORLD: this is the last card of the Major Arcana, and as such it marks the end of a cycle. This card talks about finishing a project, a happy ending, or traveling the world.

MINOR ARCANA

The Suit of Swords

1. Ace of Swords: mental clarity, a new bright idea, success.
2. Two of Swords: being divided between two options, indecision.
3. Three of Swords: sorrow, painfully letting go of something, painful but necessary loss.
4. Four of Swords: time to take a rest or be passive.
5. Five of Swords: conflict, being defeated, someone who must win at all costs.
6. Six of Swords: leaving behind something against your wishes; painful but necessary transition towards a brighter future.
7. Seven of Swords: being betrayed or lied to by someone, being defeated, a fake friend.
8. Eight of Swords: feeling trapped by your own convictions, but there is a way out if you make an effort to see the truth.
9. Nine of Swords: worrying, something which doesn't let you sleep, but you can put an end to this desperation.
10. Ten of Swords: touching rock bottom, as bad as it can get, but from here on it can only get better (the worst has come to pass, and it is over).
11. Page of Swords: the birth of a fresh idea, an intelligent child.
12. Knight of Swords: fighting for your ideals, acting on an idea, a smart but sharp-tongued young person.
13. Queen of Swords: thinking quickly and getting organized about something; an intelligent but sometimes sad woman.
14. King of Swords: being able to think clearly, seeing

the big picture and winning thanks to your intellect. An intelligent adult man.

The Suit of Pentacles

1. Ace of Pentacles: new financial or business opportunity.
2. Two of Pentacles: achieving balance, juggling work and home.
3. Three of Pentacles: time to learn something, perfect your skills, learning from a master.
4. Four of Pentacles: holding on to material things, avoiding expenses (can border on stinginess).
5. Five of Pentacles: losses, being in need of material help.
6. Six of Pentacles: giving and sharing with those less fortunate than you; receiving (financial) help.
7. Seven of Pentacles: reaping what you have sown, being rewarded for your hard work.
8. Eight of Pentacles: working hard and becoming a master of your craft.
9. Nine of Pentacles: enjoying the pleasures of life.
10. Ten of Pentacles: enjoying family life and material wealth, an inheritance, a happy retirement.
11. Page of Pentacles: a new financial or job opportunity is born; a sensible child.
12. Knight of Pentacles: working steadily towards a material goal; slow but efficient young person.
13. Queen of Pentacles: taking care of the needs of others; a motherly, down-to-earth woman.
14. King of Pentacles: financial abundance; a sensible man who is in control of his finances.

The Suit of Wands

1. Ace of Wands: inspiration, new creative beginning.
2. Two of Wands: planning for the future, starting a venture.
3. Three of Wands: good things are coming, expansion.

4. Four of Wands: creating a firm foundation, a stable home, a celebration or marriage.
5. Five of Wands: conflict or disagreement.
6. Six of Wands: victory and public recognition.
7. Seven of Wands: a struggle, standing your ground.
8. Eight of Wands: speed, a fast change, travel.
9. Nine of Wands: persisting, don't give up before the end.
10. Ten of Wands: tiredness, being burdened.
11. Page of Wands: enthusiasm, a child full of energy.
12. Knight of Wands: passion, fast travel or news, a hasty young person.
13. Queen of Wands: exuberance and decision, a determined woman who loves attention.
14. King of Wands: being passionate but in control, acting bravely but wisely, a man with such characteristics.

The Suit of Cups

1. Ace of Cups: new (positive) feelings, new love, a new beginning.
2. Two of Cups: union, love, partnership.
3. Three of Cups: celebration, a party, friend reunion.
4. Four of Cups: ungratefulness, apathy, seeing the cup half empty.
5. Five of Cups: sadness, loss, crying over something you can't change.
6. Six of Cups: childhood memories, nostalgia, being childlike.
7. Seven of Cups: choices, letting yourself be fooled by the appearances.
8. Eight of Cups: the need for solitude, leaving something dear behind.
9. Nine of Cups: happiness, wishes come true.
10. Ten of Cups: family happiness. Well-being.
11. Page of Cups: new feelings, new love, a sensitive child.
12. Knight of Cups: good news, a romantic young

person.

13. Queen of Cups: nurturing your feelings, an intuitive and loving woman.

14. King of Cups: balanced feelings, a balanced man.

Tables Of Correspondences

TYPE OF SPELL	COLORS	HERBS	SEASON	ELEMENT	DIRECTION	CRYSTALS	CHAKRA	RELATED TAROT SUIT	RELATED TAROT CARDS	MOON PHASE	NUMBER
Love (romantic, self-love), friendship	red, pink, green	pink rose, vanilla, cinnamon, lavender	Fall, Summer	Water, Fire	West, South	rose quartz, peridot, aventurine, malachite, jade	Heart	Cups	The Lovers, 2 of cups	waxing, full	2, 6, even numbers
Love (passionate)	red, orange	red rose, cinnamon	Summer	Fire	South	carnelian, garnet, red topaz, sunstone	Sacral	Wands	The Lovers, The Devil	waxing, full	2, 3, 5
Health	green, yellow, golden	coriander, geranium, lavender, rosemary, ginger	Spring	Earth	East	peridot, aventurine, malachite, jade	Heart	Pentacles	Ace of Pentacles, Temperance	waxing, full (or waning to banish)	4
Money	green, yellow, golden	bay leave, thyme, ginger, dandelion flower	Spring	Earth	East	citrine, amber, tiger's eye	Solar plexus	Pentacles	Ace of Pentacles, 10 of Pentacles	full, or waxing for growth	8, 3
Banishing	black	sage, angelica, elderberry	Winter	Air	North	black obsidian, black tourmaline, jet, apache tears, smoky quartz	Root	Depending on subject of banishing.	Death, The World, Judgement	waning	3, 8, 9

Intention	Color	Herbs	Season	Element	Direction	Crystals	Chakra	Suit	Tarot	Moon	Numbers
Protection	black	plantain, yarrow, nettle, garlic, cumin, rosemary, parsley	Fall	Water	West	black obsidian, black tourmaline, jet, apache tears, smoky quartz	Third Eye	Pentacles	Strength, Justice	waxing, full	3, 8
Intuition	indigo, dark blue	yarrow, rosemary	Fall	Water	West	sodalite, lapis lazuli	Third Eye	Cups	The High Priestess, The Moon	full moon, sometimes new moon	5, 7, 9
Good luck (general), optimism, creativity	white, orange	dandelion, clover, bay leave, rosemary	Spring, Winter	Earth, Air	East, North	citrine, amber, tiger's eye, carnelian	solar plexus	Pentacles, or depending on spell	Th Sun, Ace of Pentacles	full moon, waxing	3, 6
Motivation, courage, power	red	ginger, garlic, cinnamon	Summer	Fire	South	carnelian, garnet, red topaz	Root	Wands	The Chariot, The Emperor, King of Wands	waxing, full	1, 3, 4
Communication, peace	blue, pink, white	oregano, sage	Winter, Fall	Earth, Water	North, West	angelite, blue lace agate, turquoise	Throat	Swords	Temperance, Pages for messages.	waxing, full	2
Magic, spiritual growth	purple	frankincense, yarrow, rosemary, lavender, clove, jasmine	Spring, Fall, Winter		East, West, North	amethyst	Crown	Swords, Cups	The High Priestess, The Empress, The Magician	waxing, full, sometimes new moon	1, 3, 5, 6, 7, 9
Mental clarity, peace	white	angelica, sage	Winter	Air	North	clear quartz, calcite	Third Eye, Crown	Swords	Temperance, The High Priestess, The Star	waxing, full	2, 9

139

About The Author

Beatrix M. Linden has been fascinated with magic and Witchcraft since she was a child. A few years ago she left behind a busy corporate life and exchanged it for a frugal, minimalistic existence, surrounded by hills, cats and everlasting frost. Beatrix writes about magic, divination and other esoteric subjects, and now and then sells her art and handmade items online and at craft fairs. She owns a couple of brooms, but no dustpans, and loves to wear aprons and capes despite her neighbor's opinions on her attire.

You can find out more about her by visiting her website. You can also follow her on Instagram or subscribe to her YouTube channel.

Other Titles By The Same Author

- *The Solitary Witch's Green Journal*

- *El Libro Verde de la Bruja Solitaria*

Made in the USA
Las Vegas, NV
28 July 2021